I0759706

Saintly Bites for Children

Mixing Faith, Fun & Family Time in the Kitchen

By Shelby Siegfried

Illustrated by Ted Schluenderfritz

Liguori Publications
A Redemptorist Ministry
Catholic. Pastoral. Trusted.

Imprimi Potest: Kevin Zubel, CSsR, Provincial
Denver Province, The Redemptorists

Published by Liguori Publications, Liguori, Missouri 63057

Liguori Publications, a nonprofit corporation, is an apostolate of the Redemptorists (Redemptorists.com).

Visit Liguori.org or call 800-325-9521

Saintly Bites for Children
Shelby Siegfried

ISBN 978-0-7648-2874-4
E-ISBN: 978-0-7648-7258-7

Library of Congress Cataloging-in-Publication Data

Names: Siegfried, Shelby author | Schluenderfritz, Ted illustrator
Title: Saintly bites for children : mixing faith, fun, and family time in the kitchen / by Shelby Siegfried ; illustrated by Ted Schluenderfritz.

Description: First edition. | Liguori, MO : Liguori Publications, [2025] | Includes index. | Audience: Ages 8-12 | Audience: Grades 4-6 | Summary: "A cookbook geared toward children and young teens. The book is intended to promote family time together, cooking with children while learning about saints at the same time. The cookbook includes more than 60 recipes, each one based on a different saint and accompanied by a profile of that saint. The easy recipes help teach children about kitchen tools, cooking techniques, and measurements"-- Provided by publisher.

Identifiers: LCCN 2025023868 (print) | LCCN 2025023869 (ebook) | ISBN 9780764828744 hardcover | ISBN 9780764872587 ebook

Subjects: LCSH: Cooking--Juvenile literature | Saints--Biography--Juvenile literature | LCGFT: Cookbooks | Biographies

Classification: LCC TX652.5 .S533 2025 (print) | LCC TX652.5 (ebook) | DDC 641.5--dc23/eng/20250702

LC record available at https://lccn.loc.gov/2025023868

LC ebook record available at https://lccn.loc.gov/2025023869

29 28 27 26 25 / 5 4 3 2 1

First Edition

Printed in Canada

Cover illustration of Saints Louis Martin, Zélie Martin and Thérèse of Lisieux: Ted Schluenderfritz
Cover photos: Shutterstock
Recipe photos: Shelby Siegfried
Cover and interior design: Wendy Barnes

Contents

Introduction

Getting Ready to Cook With the Saints

We're All Called to Be Saints!

Did you know that every one of us is called to be a saint? That's right—no matter how young or old you are, no matter where you come from, you can live a life of holiness and love, just like the holy people we read about. Saints are ordinary people who loved God and others in extraordinary ways. They were kind, brave, generous, and they never gave up on doing what's right.

The saints show us that being holy isn't just for people who lived a long time ago—it's something we can all strive for every day. You don't have to perform miracles or be perfect to become a saint. Instead, try to live each day with love, kindness, and a heart open to God. Whether it's helping a friend, being patient with your family, or praying for someone in need, every little action can bring you closer to becoming a saint.

The Steps to Sainthood

While everyone in heaven is a saint, the Catholic Church recognizes some people who have lived especially holy and virtuous lives by giving them the official title of "Saint." Here's how that process works:

STEP 1
Opening the Cause for Canonization

A person can be considered for sainthood only after he or she has died. Usually, the Church waits at least five years after the person has passed away before starting the process. This waiting period allows time for careful and calm consideration. After this time, the local bishop can open an official cause for canonization. If there are no objections, the process begins, and the person is given the title "Servant of God."

STEP 2
Investigating the Life of the Servant of God

The next step is to investigate the person's life to see if he or she lived with "heroic virtue." This means the Church looks closely at how the person practiced his or her faith and goodness. The person in charge of this investigation is called the *postulator*. The postulator gathers as much information as possible, including the potential saint's writings as well as testimonies from people who knew the person. Sometimes, the postulator also looks at how the person died, especially if he or she was martyred for the faith.

STEP 3
Recognizing Venerable Status

Next, the postulator summarizes all of the information into a file called a *positio*. The bishop then submits the positio to the Dicastery for the Causes of the Saints in Rome. Theologians review the positio and vote to approve or deny the cause for sainthood. If the Church finds that the person lived a life of great faith and virtue, he or she is given the title "Venerable." This shows that the Church recognizes this person's holiness.

STEP 4
Beatification as Blessed

The next step is beatification, in which the person receives the title "Blessed." For this to happen, something miraculous usually needs to be attributed to the *intercession* of the person, which means that praying to this person has caused a *miracle*; for example, the healing of someone who is very sick. This shows that he or she is in heaven and can intercede—or pray directly to God—for us. All potential miracles are reviewed through a strict process to prove that they are authentic, or true, miracles that cannot be explained by science. If the Church approves the miracle, the pope declares the Venerable as Blessed. If the person is a martyr, meaning they died for their Catholic faith, then a miracle is not required for beatification.

STEP 5
Canonization as a Saint

The final step is canonization, in which the person is officially declared a saint. This usually requires another verified miracle. When someone is canonized, the Church declares that they are in heaven, and we can publicly honor them and ask for their prayers.

Remember, you don't have to wait until you're older to start living like a saint. Every kind word, every good deed, and every prayer brings you closer to God and helps you grow in holiness. So, let's try our best every day to follow the example of the saints and live lives full of love, joy, and faith. Who knows? One day, you might be a saint too!

HOLY HEROES Table Talk

The saints were ordinary people who did extraordinary things because of their deep love for God and others. After making a recipe, share what you've learned with your family around the dinner table. Use the following questions to discover how the saints can guide us in our everyday lives. Whether it's a simple act of kindness or a big step in faith, there's always something we can learn from the saints!

1. What did you find most inspiring about this saint's story?
2. How did this saint show his or her love for God in daily life?
3. What challenges did this saint face, and how did he or she overcome them with faith?
4. How can we apply the lessons from this saint's life to our own lives?
5. What virtues did this saint practice that we can try to practice too?
6. How did this saint help others, and what can we do to help those around us?
7. If you could ask this saint for advice, what would you want to know?
8. Which of this saint's qualities do you admire most, and why?
9. How did this saint's faith help him or her in difficult times?
10. How do you see examples of this saint in people you know?

Before You Begin

Saintly Safety Tips

Cooking is a lot of fun, especially when you learn from the saints! Before you start making something tasty, here are some important tips to keep you safe and help you become a great chef.

1. Ask for Help: Even the saints knew when to ask for help. Always ask an adult to assist you in the kitchen. Whether you're chopping, boiling, or baking, having an extra pair of hands can make things easier and safer.

2. Tie Back Long Hair: Just like St. Kateri braided her hair, make sure to tie your hair back and roll up long sleeves so they don't get in the food. This keeps everything neat and clean.

3. Wear an Apron: Saint Martha was known for her hospitality and taking care of the home. Put on an apron to keep your clothes clean while you cook, just like she would.

4. Keep it Clean: Cleanliness is very important! Wash your hands before you start cooking and make sure that your work surfaces are clean.

5. Read the Recipe First: Saint Benedict taught the importance of being prepared, so read through the entire recipe before you begin. This way, you will know what to expect and what tools and ingredients you need to get ready.

6. Gather Your Ingredients and Tools: Have all your ingredients and tools ready to go on your work surface or nearby. This will make cooking easier and more fun.

7. Work Safely: Saints were careful and thoughtful in their work, and you should be too. Be careful with knives, hot stoves, and ovens. Ask an adult to help you with anything that might be tricky or dangerous.

8. Clean as You Go: Many saints loved simplicity and order for tasks big and small. Keep your workspace organized by cleaning surfaces and putting things away when you finish using them. This will help you enjoy your time in the kitchen!

9. Keep Cooking: A saint is a sinner who keeps trying, and a chef is a cook who keeps cooking! If something doesn't quite turn out like you hoped, don't give up—try again!

10. Have Fun: Remember, cooking is a way to share love with others, just like the saints did. Enjoy the process and don't be afraid to ask questions or try something new.

Cooking with the saints can be a wonderful adventure, so let's get started and make something delicious!

Common Ingredients

Here are some ingredients you'll see in many of the recipes in this book. You probably even have many of these in your pantry right now.

Baking powder

When mixed into dough or batter, baking powder releases gas bubbles that helps baked goods rise and become fluffy during baking.

Baking soda

Baking soda also helps baked goods rise, like baking powder, but it works in a different way. Even though they do similar jobs, baking soda is not the same as baking powder, so be sure to read the recipe carefully!

Butter

Like oil, butter can be an ingredient or can be used to grease a pan. If a recipe does not tell you whether to use salted or unsalted butter, the general rule is to use unsalted butter. You can always add more salt later if needed!

Eggs

Eggs are used in many types of recipes. Eggs come in different sizes, but large eggs are the most popular size for cooking and baking.

Flour

All-purpose flour works in any recipe that calls for flour, unless the recipe lists a specific type of flour. It's good to have all-purpose flour in your pantry, because you will need it for many of these recipes.

Garlic

Garlic is a very popular and flavorful ingredient for seasoning. A head, or bulb, of garlic is made of individual segments, or cloves. Some recipes will tell you how many cloves to use, while other recipes use minced garlic or dried garlic powder.

Herbs

Herbs are either fresh (usually in the produce section of the grocery store) or dried (in shaker bottles). Fresh herbs are much more flavorful than dried, so recipes often need only small amounts of fresh herbs. The recipe will tell you if you should use fresh or dried herbs.

Milk

Some recipes in this book need a certain type of milk, such as whole milk. However, if the type of milk is not given, you can usually use either low-fat milk or whole milk. For baking, you can even substitute nondairy milk, such as soy or coconut, and get similar results.

Oil

Different types of oils are used in cooking. Sometimes oil is an ingredient in the recipe; sometimes it is used to grease a pan that you will cook or bake in. Oils used in these recipes include olive oil, avocado oil, and vegetable oil.

Onions

There are many types of onions, such as white onions, red onions, green onions, and more. Some recipes call for larger pieces of sliced onions, and other recipes use chopped onions to add flavor to the dish.

Pepper

Salt often has a partner: pepper! When a recipe calls for "pepper," it means ground black pepper (think of a pepper shaker). If a different type of pepper is needed, such as cracked pepper or cayenne pepper, it will be clearly mentioned in the recipe.

Salt

There are many kinds of salt. For most of the recipes that use salt, regular table salt is fine. If a different type of salt, such as sea salt (which has larger crystals) is needed, the recipe will tell you.

Spices

Ground spices let you quickly add flavor to a recipe. They usually come in plastic shaker bottles or glass jars. If you keep them tightly closed, they should be good for up to one year.

Sugar

In these recipes, if "sugar" is listed as an ingredient, it means granulated white sugar. That is the type of sugar most commonly used for the recipes in this book. Some recipes call for brown sugar, which comes in light or dark, or confectioners' (powdered) sugar.

Measuring Your Ingredients and Common Conversions

Did you know that dry ingredients and liquid ingredients are measured differently? While it's OK to use measuring spoons for both dry and liquid ingredients, larger amounts need different types of measuring cups.

For liquid ingredients (such as oil or water), use a clear plastic or glass measuring cup with a spout and a handle. The cup will be marked with lines to show you the different amounts. Try to find a large measuring cup that holds up to 2 cups. To measure, fill the measuring cup carefully up to the line that marks the amount you need. Then, you can easily pour the liquid into a mixing bowl or pan.

Measuring cups for dry ingredients (such as sugar, flour, or rice) come in sets that include a variety of cups in different sizes (for example, ¼ cup, 1/3 cup, ½ cup, and 1 cup). These cups have handles so you can scoop up ingredients. Make sure that the measuring cup is level, not overfilled or underfilled, before pouring the ingredient into the mixing bowl or pan.

Quick Tips

Remember these conversions that will make measuring easier:

3 teaspoons = 1 tablespoon

16 tablespoons = 1 cup

16 ounces = 1 pound

Here are some helpful measurement conversions.

Dry Measurements

3 teaspoons = 1 tablespoon = 1/16 cup

6 teaspoons = 2 tablespoons = 1/8 cup

12 teaspoons = 4 tablespoons = 1/4 cup

24 teaspoons = 8 tablespoons = 1/2 cup

36 teaspoons = 12 tablespoons = 3/4 cup

48 teaspoons = 16 tablespoons = 1 cup

Liquid Measurements

8 fluid ounces = 1 cup = 1/2 pint = 1/4 quart

16 fluid ounces = 2 cups = 1 pint = 1/2 quart

32 fluid ounces = 4 cups = 2 pints = 1 quart = 1/4 gallon

128 fluid ounces = 16 cups = 8 pints = 4 quarts = 1 gallon

US to Metric Volume Conversions

1 teaspoon = 5 milliliters

2 teaspoon = 10 milliliters

1 tablespoon = 15 milliliters

2 tablespoon = 30 milliliters

1/4 cup = 59 milliliters

1/3 cup = 79 milliliters

1/2 cup = 118 milliliters

3/4 cup = 177 milliliters

1 cup = 237 milliliters

2 cups = 1 pint = 473 milliliters

4 cups = 1 quart = 0.946 liter

4 quarts = 1 gallon = 3.8 liters

US to Metric Weight Conversions

½ ounce = 14 grams

¾ ounce = 21 grams

1 ounce = 28 grams

2 ounces = 57 grams

3 ounces = 85 grams

4 ounces = 113 grams

5 ounces = 142 grams

6 ounces = 170 grams

8 ounces = 227 grams

10 ounces = 283 grams

12 ounces = 340 grams

16 ounces = 1 pound = 454 grams

Fahrenheit to Celsius Temperature Conversions

250°F = 120°C

300°F = 150°C

325°F = 165°C

350°F = 180°C

375°F = 190°C

400°F = 200°C

425°F = 220°C

450°F = 245°C

Safe Minimum Internal Temperature for Meat

Beef, pork, veal, and lamb steaks, chops, and roasts: 145°F (62.8°C) (allow meat to rest for at least 3 minutes before taking temperature)

All poultry 165°F (73.9°C)

Safe steps in food handling, cooking, and storage are essential in preventing foodborne illness. You can't see, smell, or taste harmful bacteria that may cause illness. In every step of food preparation, follow these four guidelines to keep food safe:

Clean—Wash hands and surfaces often.

Separate—Separate raw meat from other foods.

Cook—Cook to the right temperature.

Chill—Refrigerate food promptly.

Cook all food to the recommended minimum internal temperatures, as measured with a food thermometer, before removing food from the heat source. For reasons of personal preference, you may choose to cook food to higher temperatures.

Get to Know Your Tools

Take a look at some of the common tools you will use while preparing the ingredients and making the recipes.

Large
Saucepan
Skillet
Rolling Pin
Rimmed Baking Sheet
Muffin Tin
Pastry Brush
Pie Plate or Pie Tin
Oven Mitts
Wire Cooling Rack
Dry Measuring Cups
Box
Grater
Food Thermometer
Vegetable
Peeler
Potato Masher
Rubber
Spatula
Colander
Ladle

Glossary of Terms Used in This Book

Beat: To mix quickly, usually with a whisk or electric mixer, to combine the ingredients well and to add air into the mixture for a light and fluffy texture.

Boil: To heat liquid until it is bubbling and has reached a temperature of 212°F (100°C), or to cook food in boiling water.

Broil: To cook at a high temperature, usually in the oven, with the heat source directly above the food.

Chop: To cut food with a knife into small pieces.

Grate: To make very small pieces of food by running it over the small, sharp holes of a grater. Cheese and vegetables are commonly grated foods.

Grill: To cook food on a metal rack directly over the heat source—think of a barbecue.

Melt: To cause a solid food, such as chocolate or butter, to turn into liquid by heating it.

Mince: To cut food with a knife into tiny pieces, smaller than chopping.

Peel: To remove the outer layer of food, such as the skin or rind of a fruit or vegetable.

Sauté: To cook food in a shallow pan in a small amount of fat, such as butter or oil.

Scrape: To use a tool, such as a rubber spatula, to push ingredients on the sides of a bowl (pan, food processor, etc.) back into the bottom of the bowl with the rest of the mixture.

Shred: To cut food into small, narrow pieces, often by using the larger holes on a box grater.

Simmer: To heat liquid until small bubbles form and the temperature is just below boiling, or to cook food in simmering liquid.

Slice: To cut food with a knife into flat, often thin, pieces (think of slicing a cucumber or a loaf of bread) or individual portions (think of slicing a cake).

Stir: To use a tool such as a spoon or spatula to mix ingredients together, usually in a bowl, pan, or glass.

Toast: To heat food, usually in a toaster, pan, or oven, until it is golden brown.

Toss: To gently combine ingredients with tongs or two forks and/or spoons in order to distribute the ingredients evenly. You toss salad in a bowl (you don't stir it).

Whip: Similar to beating; to mix quickly to add air to a mixture of ingredients or a single ingredient (such as cream, to make whipped cream).

Whisk: To use a whisk to combine ingredients into a uniform, well-blended mixture.

Zest: To remove the flavorful colored outer peel (called the zest) from a lemon, lime, or orange with a zester, grater, or peeler. The zest does not include the white skin (called the pith) underneath the colorful peel.

Breakfast and Brunch

"God hugs you.
You are encircled by the arms
of the mystery of God."

Saint Hildegard of Bingen

Saint Hildegard of Bingen

Healing Foods of Joy

1098–1179 * Feast day: September 17

Patron of ecology, musicians, and writers

Hildegard was a remarkable woman whose life was filled with wonder and talent. Born in 1098 in the small village of Bermersheim vor der Höhe in Germany, she began having visions from God when she was just three years old. These special experiences made her feel very close to God, and she wanted to share his love and wisdom with everyone.

Hildegard did many different things. She was a mystic, healer, artist, scientist, composer, poet, writer, philosopher, and theologian. She even became the leader of a group of nuns. Despite being born into a noble family, she chose to dedicate her life to God and helping others.

One of the most amazing things about Hildegard was her knowledge of healing. She believed that God's creations, like plants and foods, had the power to heal and bring joy. She wrote many books about the natural world and how different plants and foods could make us healthy and happy. She called these "foods of joy."

One of her favorite grains was spelt. She found spelt to be warm and gentle on the stomach, and she believed it made people strong, healthy, and cheerful. This recipe includes spelt plus some other favorite ingredients of the saint: spices! Hildegard believed eating warm spices, like nutmeg and cinnamon, would make us joyful—and what better way to start the day?

Saint Hildegard of Bingen, pray for us!

Spiced Spelt Pancakes

Ingredients

(SERVES 6 TO 8)

1 cup spelt flour
1 tablespoon sugar
½ teaspoon baking powder
½ teaspoon baking soda
¼ teaspoon salt
¼ teaspoon nutmeg
¼ teaspoon cinnamon
¾ cups buttermilk
¼ cup milk
1 egg
Nonstick cooking spray

Tools Checklist

Measuring cups
Measuring spoons
Large bowl
Mixing spoons
Griddle
Spatula

Instructions

1. Mix together the flour, sugar, baking powder, baking soda, salt, nutmeg, and cinnamon in a large mixing bowl.
2. Stir in the buttermilk, milk, and egg until the batter is well combined.
3. Heat a griddle over medium heat and lightly coat the surface with cooking spray.
4. Pour ¼ cup of batter for each pancake onto the griddle.
5. Cook until bubbles form on the surface, then flip and cook until both sides are golden brown.
6. Serve hot from the griddle with your favorite toppings.

Saint Patrick

The Brave Shepherd of Ireland

387–461 * Feast day: March 17

Patron of Ireland, migrants, and engineers

One day, while walking along the beach in western Great Britain, sixteen-year-old Patrick was captured by pirates! They took him to Ireland and sold him as a slave. Patrick had to work hard in the fields, tending sheep, and he missed his family terribly. But he never lost hope. He prayed to God every day. One day, he heard God's voice telling him to escape. Patrick bravely ran to the sea and found a ship ready to take him home.

After returning home to Britain, Patrick couldn't forget the people of Ireland. He felt God calling him back to teach them about Christ. He spent many years studying, and he became a priest and finally a bishop. When he was ready, he returned to Ireland—not as a slave, but as a missionary.

Patrick traveled all over Ireland, sharing his message. Many people were angry with him because he was teaching a new faith, and they often tried to stop him. But Patrick's courage and faith were unshakable.

He used the shamrock, a small green clover with three leaves, to explain the Holy Trinity: God as the Father, the Son, and the Holy Spirit. The people of Ireland began to love him for his kindness and his way of making complicated ideas simple.

Saint Patrick's virtues of faith, hope, charity, justice, and determination made him a hero. He overcame many obstacles to bring his message to the Irish people. He started hundreds of churches and inspired countless hearts with his bravery and dedication.

To celebrate St. Patrick's incredible journey and his love for the people of Ireland, enjoy this hearty Irish Green Breakfast Casserole. Packed with potatoes, sausage, and green spinach, this dish will energize you for the adventures ahead, just as Patrick's faith nourished the people of Ireland. Remember St. Patrick's story and let him inspire you to be brave and trust God's will for your own life.

Saint Patrick, pray for us!

Irish Green Breakfast Casserole

Ingredients

(SERVES 6 TO 8)

Nonstick cooking spray
1 pound loose breakfast sausage
2 cups roughly chopped spinach
1 (32-ounce) bag frozen hash brown potatoes
8 large eggs
1 cup heavy cream
½ cup milk
1 teaspoon garlic powder
½ teaspoon paprika
Pinch ground sage
1 teaspoon kosher salt
½ teaspoon ground white pepper
1 cup shredded sharp cheddar cheese

Tools Checklist

9 x 13-inch baking dish
Knife
Skillet
Mixing spoons
Measuring cups
Measuring spoons
Large bowl
Whisk
Oven mitts

Instructions

1. Preheat the oven to 375°F. Coat the bottom of a 9 x 13-inch baking dish with nonstick cooking spray.
2. In a large skillet, cook the sausage over medium heat until browned, breaking it up with the side of a spoon. When the sausage is fully cooked, stir in the hash browns and cook until the potatoes are tender, stirring occasionally. Add the chopped spinach and continue cooking until the leaves are just wilted.
3. In a large bowl, whisk together the eggs, cream, milk, garlic powder, paprika, sage, salt, and pepper. Then, whisk in the cheddar. Stir in the sausage/potato/spinach mixture.
4. Pour the mixture into the prepared baking dish.
5. Bake until the top is browned and the center is set, about 45 minutes.
6. Remove from the oven and serve warm. Store leftovers in a covered container in the refrigerator for up to two days.

Saint Francis de Sales

The Gentle Teacher

1567–1622 * Feast day: January 24

Patron of authors, journalists, writers, deaf people, and educators

Saint Francis de Sales was born in a grand castle in the Savoy region of France, not far from Geneva, Switzerland, to a noble family. From a young age, Francis felt a strong calling to serve God, but he kept it a secret for years because his father wanted him to become a lawyer.

One day, while riding his horse, Francis had a remarkable experience. He fell off his horse three times, and each time, his sword and scabbard landed on the ground in the shape of a cross. This sign from God gave Francis the courage to follow his true calling. He became a priest and later the bishop of Geneva.

Francis wanted to bring people back to the Catholic faith but faced many challenges. For three years, in all types of weather, he knocked on doors as he traveled on foot throughout the Swiss countryside. Most people would not listen to what he had to say, but Francis had the patience and determination to keep working.

He decided he needed to find a different way to get people to pay attention to his message. So, he started writing about the Catholic faith and slipping the pages under people's doors.

Francis also loved children. He would play with them, and soon their parents began to see his kind heart and listen to his teachings. Through his gentle persistence, Francis brought thousands of people back to the Church.

Saint Francis de Sales taught that everyone, no matter their job or family situation, could lead a holy life. He wrote a famous book, *Introduction to the Devout Life*, to help ordinary people grow in their faith.

To celebrate St. Francis's kindness and persistence, enjoy these Mini Blueberry Muffins. They are small and simple but full of sweetness, just like his words. Remember St. Francis de Sales and his message that everyone can live a holy life, one small act of love at a time.

Saint Francis de Sales, pray for us!

Mini Blueberry Muffins

Ingredients

(MAKES 24)

Butter or nonstick cooking spray
1 cup all-purpose flour
½ cup brown sugar
1 teaspoon baking powder
¼ teaspoon cinnamon
¼ teaspoon salt
1 egg
½ cup milk
2 tablespoons butter, melted
½ cup blueberries

Tools Checklist

24-cup mini-muffin pan
Measuring cups
Measuring spoons
Small and large bowls
Mixing spoons
Whisk
Oven mitts
Wire cooling rack

Instructions

1. Heat the oven to 375°F. Lightly grease the bottom of a 24-cup mini-muffin pan with butter or cooking spray.
2. In a small mixing bowl, stir together the flour, brown sugar, baking powder, cinnamon, and salt.
3. In a bigger bowl, whisk together the egg, milk, and melted butter.
4. Stir the flour mixture into the egg mixture just until all the ingredients are wet. Gently mix the blueberries into the batter.
5. Spoon the batter into the prepared pan until the muffin cups are about 2/3 full.
6. Bake until a toothpick comes out clean when inserted into the center, about 12 minutes.
7. Let the baked muffins cool in the pan for 2 to 3 minutes before turning them out onto a wire cooling rack.

Note: For regular-sized muffins, use a 12-cup muffin pan and bake for 15 to 18 minutes.

Saint Benedict

A Man of Prayer and Work

480–547 * Feast day: July 11

Patron of students and Europe

In the hills of Nursia, Italy, twins were born around 480. Their names were Benedict and Scholastica, and they both grew up to become saints! Young Benedict was sent to Rome to study. But he found the city to be very rowdy, and many of the other students were behaving sinfully. So, Benedict left Rome, gave up his inheritance, and went to live in a small village. When God called him to an even deeper solitude, he moved to a cave in the mountains and lived alone for three years, dedicating his life to God.

People soon heard about Benedict's holiness and wisdom. Monks from a nearby monastery asked him to be their leader. But these monks didn't want to follow Benedict's strict rules, and some even tried to poison his drink! When Benedict blessed the poisoned cup, it shattered, and he was saved.

Benedict's life was marked by education, prayer, penitence, and miracles. Once, when the monks ran out of food, Benedict prayed, and a basket of bread miraculously appeared at the door. Another time, a large stone the monks needed for building wouldn't budge, but after Benedict prayed, they were able to move it easily.

The rules Benedict wrote for his monks are still used today. The most famous phrase from these rules is *ora et labora* ("prayer and work"). Benedict taught his monks to find God in their daily work and to treat everyone with kindness and respect.

To celebrate St. Benedict's dedication and faith, enjoy this Overnight Eggs Benedict Casserole. This dish requires patience and care, and the result is delicious and satisfying. Whether you're cooking, studying, or doing chores, remember St. Benedict's lessons of faith, perseverance, and finding holiness in everyday tasks.

Saint Benedict, pray for us!

Overnight Eggs Benedict Casserole

Ingredients (SERVES 12)

For the casserole:

Nonstick cooking spray
6 English muffins
1 pound Canadian bacon
10 large eggs
1 cup milk, preferably whole milk
1 teaspoon salt
¾ teaspoon black pepper
Chives, for garnish (optional)

For the Hollandaise sauce:

1½ sticks (¾ cup) unsalted butter
6 large egg yolks
2½ tablespoons lemon juice
½ teaspoon salt
Splash of hot sauce or pinch of ground cayenne pepper, if desired

Tools Checklist

9 x 13-inch baking dish
Knives
Measuring cups
Measuring spoons
Large and small bowls
Mixing spoons
Whisk
Foil or plastic wrap
Oven mitts
Blender

Instructions

For the casserole:

1. Spray a 9 x 13-inch baking dish with nonstick cooking spray.
2. Split the English muffins in half, then dice into ½-inch cubes. Place the cubes in the bottom of the prepared baking dish.
3. Cube the Canadian bacon, then add half of it on top of the bread. Toss the bread and meat cubes together, then spread the mixture evenly in the bottom of the pan.
4. In a large mixing bowl, whisk together the eggs, milk, salt, and black pepper until evenly combined.
5. Pour the egg mixture into the baking dish and top with the remaining meat cubes. Press down on the meat to make sure it is all covered by the egg mixture.

Instructions continued on next page.

6. Cover the baking dish with aluminum foil or plastic wrap and refrigerate overnight (or up to 24 hours).
7. About 30 minutes before baking, take the baking dish out of the refrigerator and let it sit at room temperature, covered.
8. Preheat the oven to 350°F.
9. Remove the foil or plastic wrap and bake for 50 minutes to 1 hour, until the eggs are set. Place a loose piece of foil over the dish during the last 20 minutes of baking to avoid over-browning.
10. Remove from the oven and keep covered until ready to serve and slice.

For the Hollandaise sauce:

1. Melt the butter and set it aside. It should still be warm when blending the sauce.
2. Place the egg yolks, lemon juice, salt, and splash of hot sauce or pinch of cayenne pepper (if desired) into a blender and blend on high for just a few seconds.
3. Blend on low while very slowly streaming in the warm melted butter. The sauce will begin thickening. Taste and adjust seasoning if needed.
4. Serve immediately by pouring the sauce over the individual slices of the casserole, followed by a sprinkle of chives, if desired.

Whether you're cooking, studying, or doing chores, remember St. Benedict's lessons of faith, perseverance, and finding holiness in everyday tasks.

Saint Teresa of Ávila

The Courageous Reformer

1515–1582 * Feast day: October 15

Patron of Spain, lacemakers, those in need of grace, those in religious orders, and those ridiculed for their piety

Teresa was a lively young woman who lived in the town of Ávila in central Spain. She enjoyed love stories, gossip, clothes, and rebelling against rules. When she was sixteen, her father decided that her behavior was out of control, so he sent her to a convent. Even though she didn't want to be a nun at first, she eventually enjoyed the convent and later joined the Carmelites. This wealthy convent allowed her to keep her social life, and Teresa found it too easy to slip into a worldly life and ignore God. For almost twenty years, Teresa was not too serious about being a nun. She wanted to be close to God, but she found it hard.

Everything changed when she prayed before a statue of Christ. Teresa committed herself to pursuing a life of spiritual perfection. She felt very close to God from then on and had many special experiences. She saw Jesus and angels and even had moments in heaven. People said she sometimes floated in the air when she prayed!

Teresa decided to change the Carmelite order to be more focused on prayer and simplicity. She bravely traveled across Spain, starting new convents for nuns to live simply and support each other. Many people didn't like what she was doing, but her strong faith kept her going.

Teresa wanted her nuns to live by three important rules: love others, don't be too attached to things, and be humble. She also believed in having a sense of humor and being patient and kind to each other, just like in a family.

Saint Teresa of Ávila was the first of only four women to be named a doctor of the Church. She shaped many religious communities, and her writings on the soul's journey to God has inspired generations.

Just as St. Teresa turned spiritual dryness into holiness, this Pan de Santa Teresa transforms stale bread into a sweet treat full of Spanish flavors.

Saint Teresa of Ávila, pray for us!

Pan de Santa Teresa

Ingredients

(SERVES 6)

3 cups whole milk

2 tablespoons honey

2 tablespoons sugar, plus more for sprinkling

1 cinnamon stick (or ½ teaspoon ground cinnamon), plus more for sprinkling

2 wide strips lemon peel or orange peel, or 1 of each

6 thick slices stale bread

2 large eggs

Extra-virgin olive oil, for pan frying

Extra honey, for drizzling (optional)

Tools Checklist

Medium saucepan

Mixing spoons

Shallow baking dish or rimmed sheet pan

Wide, shallow bowl

Spatula or tongs

Instructions

1. In a medium saucepan over medium heat, bring the milk, honey, sugar, cinnamon stick, and citrus peels to a simmer. Once simmering, remove the pan from the heat and let the mixture cool until lukewarm, about 30 minutes. Stir occasionally to prevent skin from forming. Remove the cinnamon stick and citrus peels when the mixture has cooled.
2. Arrange the bread slices in a single layer in a large, shallow dish or a small, rimmed sheet pan. Pour the cooled milk mixture over the bread slices, then let rest until the bread has soaked up all of the milk, about 30 minutes.
3. Beat the eggs in a wide, shallow bowl. In a large nonstick pan over medium heat, heat enough olive oil to coat the bottom of the pan.
4. Gently remove one slice of bread from the dish, dip both sides in the beaten egg, then place it in the hot pan to fry. Cook until golden, 1 to 2 minutes on each side.
5. Continue with the remaining slices of bread, frying one or two slices at a time, depending on the size of the pan.
6. Serve warm with a generous sprinkling of cinnamon and sugar. Add a drizzle of honey if desired.

Saint Nicholas of Flüe

Protector of Switzerland

1417–1487 * Feast day: March 21

Patron of Switzerland and Pontifical Swiss Guard

As a young man, Nicholas was a brave soldier, fighting in important battles to protect his country of Switzerland. Tradition says he fought with a sword in one hand and a rosary in the other! He served in the military from the ages of twenty-one to thirty-seven, even becoming a captain.

After leaving the army, Nicholas married and became a farmer, councilor, and judge in his community. He was known for his wisdom and fairness. But Nicholas felt a deeper calling. After receiving a vision from God, he decided to leave politics and devote himself to his faith.

In 1467, with the consent of his wife and ten grown children, Nicholas became a hermit at the age of fifty. He built a small hut from branches and leaves not far from his home, and he lived a very simple life. He didn't wear a cap or shoes, even in the winter. Amazingly, Nicholas lived without any food but the holy Eucharist for the rest of his life.

People from all over Europe came to Switzerland to seek his advice. Known simply as Brother Klaus, Nicholas was kind and wise, helping many people. One of his greatest achievements was helping to unite Switzerland and prevent a civil war. His guidance and wisdom brought peace to the land.

Nicholas is the patron saint of the Swiss Guards, who have protected the pope since 1506. The Swiss Guards are known for their colorful uniforms and bravery.

This Swiss and Spinach Quiche invites us to celebrate Switzerland's heritage of unity, hospitality, and delicious Swiss cheese! As we enjoy these flavors from his homeland, we can be inspired by St. Nicholas' role in guiding and uniting his country, and we can pray for all who guard and protect others with dedication, just as the Swiss Guards carry on his legacy of faithfulness and service today.

Saint Nicholas of Flüe, pray for us!

Swiss and Spinach Quiche

Tools Checklist

9-inch pie plate
Knives
Cheese grater
Measuring cups and Measuring spoons
Baking sheet
Large sauté pan
Spatula
Large bowl
Whisk
Mixing spoons

Ingredients (SERVES 6 TO 8)

2 tablespoons salted butter
1/3 cup finely diced white onion
12 ounces (about 4 cups) baby bella mushrooms, sliced
2 cups (about 2 ounces) baby spinach
6 large eggs
1 cup heavy cream
1 teaspoon garlic powder
1 teaspoon kosher salt
1 teaspoon freshly ground black pepper
12 ounces Swiss cheese, grated
1 homemade or store-bought 9-inch pie crust, unbaked

Instructions

1. Preheat the oven to 350°F.
2. Fit the pie crust into a 9-inch pie plate. Fold the edges of the crust under the edges of the pie plate and crimp as desired, then set the pie plate on a baking sheet. (This will make it easier to move once you fill it.)
3. In a large sauté pan, heat the butter over medium heat until melted. Add the onion and sauté until tender, about 6 minutes. Add the mushrooms and sauté until their liquid has mostly evaporated, 5 to 6 minutes. Add the spinach and sauté until wilted, 1 to 2 minutes. Remove from the heat and set aside.

Instructions continued on next page.

4. In a large bowl, whisk together the eggs, cream, garlic powder, salt, and pepper. Stir in the spinach/mushroom mixture and the Swiss cheese. Pour the mixture into the unbaked pie crust.
5. Bake until the quiche is light golden and set in the center (test by gently moving the pan), about 45 minutes. If the crust is browning too quickly, cover it with foil to prevent it from burning.
6. Remove from the oven and let stand for 5 to 10 minutes before serving. Cut into 6 or 8 slices and serve warm or at room temperature.

Store leftovers in the refrigerator for up to 2 days.

As we enjoy these flavors from his homeland, we can be inspired by Saint Nicholas' role in guiding and uniting his country.

Saint Junipero Serra

The Missionary Explorer

1713–1784 * Feast day: July 1

Patron of California and vocations

Imagine leaving your home and traveling across the ocean to a new world! That's exactly what St. Junipero Serra did. Born on Spain's island of Mallorca, he became a Franciscan friar and took the name "Junipero" after a kind and simple friar he admired. He spent many years as a student and professor of theology, becoming famous for his preaching.

But Junipero had a burning desire to be a missionary. He gave up his comfortable life at age 35 and set sail for Mexico. He faced many challenges, like learning new languages and getting used to different cultures, but his strong faith and sense of adventure kept him going.

In 1769, Father Serra began his most exciting work: starting missions in California. He traveled hundreds of miles, often on foot, to set up twenty-one missions along the coast. These missions were places where Native Americans could learn about Christianity, go to school, and learn how to farm. Father Serra cared deeply for the people he served, and he worked hard to help them.

Father Serra was known for his great love and dedication. Even with an injured leg, he walked long distances. He faced many difficulties but always trusted God's plan. He once said, "Always forward, never back."

Saint Junipero Serra teaches us about perseverance, kindness, and sharing God's love with others. His life was a journey of faith and service, always trying to help those in need. To celebrate St. Junipero Serra's inspiring life, enjoy these Pumpkin Corn Cakes, made with ingredients grown by Native Americans at the California missions.

Saint Junipero Serra, pray for us!

Pumpkin Corn Cakes

Ingredients

(MAKES 25)

1½ cups all-purpose flour
1 cup cornmeal
½ cup brown sugar
1 tablespoon baking powder
½ teaspoon salt
½ teaspoon ground cinnamon
1¼ cups milk
1 cup canned pumpkin puree
2 eggs, beaten
2 tablespoons melted butter
1 teaspoon vanilla extract
1 tablespoon avocado or olive oil

Tools Checklist

Measuring cups
Measuring spoons
2 large bowls
Whisk
Mixing spoons
Griddle
Spatula

Instructions

1. Whisk the flour, cornmeal, brown sugar, baking powder, salt, and cinnamon together in a large bowl. Beat the milk, pumpkin, eggs, butter, and vanilla extract together in another bowl. Add the milk mixture to the flour mixture and stir until the batter is well combined.
2. Heat about 1 tablespoon of oil on a griddle over medium-high heat. Drop the batter by large spoonfuls onto the griddle and cook until bubbles form and the edges are dry, 3 to 4 minutes. Flip and cook until browned on the other side, 2 to 3 minutes. Repeat with remaining batter.
3. Serve warm with your favorite toppings, such as butter, maple syrup, or jam.

Venerable Fulton Sheen

The Television Priest

1895–1979 * Feast day: December 9

Patron of media and evangelization

Born in 1895 in a small town in Illinois, Fulton Sheen grew up with a strong faith and a love for learning. Even as a child, Fulton knew he wanted to be a priest. After many years of studying, he finally became a priest in 1919.

But Fulton Sheen wasn't just any priest—he had a special talent for speaking, and he loved sharing the teachings of Jesus with as many people as possible. He became famous for his radio and television shows, where he talked about faith in a way that was easy to understand and full of hope. His TV show, *Life Is Worth Living*, was watched by millions of people each week, making him one of the most well-known and beloved Catholic figures of his time.

Fulton Sheen was great at delivering short, powerful messages that stuck with people long after they heard them. He knew how to explain even the most difficult ideas in simple ways that everyone could understand. His words were like little bites of wisdom that fed people's souls and helped them feel closer to God.

Even though he became famous, Venerable Fulton Sheen stayed humble and always wanted to serve others. He traveled around the world, giving talks and writing books that still inspire people today. His life shows us how important it is to have faith and share God's love with everyone we meet.

To remember Venerable Fulton Sheen and his bite-sized wisdom, enjoy these Bacon Breakfast Bites. Just as his simple yet thoughtful words brought hope and joy to many people, these hearty bites will give you a nourishing way to start your day.

Venerable Fulton Sheen, pray for us!

LIFE IS WORTH LIVING!

Bacon Breakfast Bites

Ingredients

(MAKES 12)

6 slices bacon, cut in half

12 eggs

Salt and pepper, to taste

½ cup shredded cheddar cheese

Tools Checklist

Knife

12-cup muffin pan

Measuring cups

Oven mitts

Instructions

1. Preheat the oven to 400°F.
2. Place one slice of bacon in each cup of a 12-cup muffin pan, placing the bacon in a circle around the sides of the cup.
3. Bake the bacon for 10 minutes.
4. Remove the bacon from the oven. Crack 1 egg into each of the cups, then sprinkle with salt, pepper, and cheddar cheese.
5. Bake for another 10 minutes or until the egg yolks reach your desired consistency.
6. Run a knife around the edge of each cup to loosen and remove, then serve.

Saint Margaret of Scotland

The Queen of Kindness

1045–1093 * Feast day: November 16

Patron of the poor, the orphaned, the widowed, and the sick

Margaret was an English princess who grew up in exile in Hungary. As a child, she developed a great love of reading and prayer, and she learned all about the duties of being a princess. One day, while Margaret and her family were traveling by sea, a storm forced them to go ashore in Scotland. There, King Malcolm III welcomed and protected them, and he soon fell deeply in love with the beautiful and kind princess. Before long, Margaret and Malcolm married, making Margaret the queen of Scotland.

As queen, Margaret used her position to help others. She and King Malcolm had eight children, and Margaret made sure they were raised with love and strong faith. She worked hard to improve the lives of the Scottish people and was known for her generosity. Margaret brought clothes and food to the needy people of Scotland. She nursed the sick and even brought homeless people into the castle.

Margaret also brought positive changes to the Church in Scotland. She helped rebuild churches and monasteries and encouraged people to live good, Christian lives. Her love for God and others made a big difference in the country.

Despite being a queen, she lived a simple life and made time daily for prayer and reading Scripture. Saint Margaret's life teaches us about kindness, generosity, and faith. She showed that even in a position of power, one can live humbly and serve others.

To celebrate St. Margaret's inspiring life, enjoy these Petite Scottish Scones. Just as Margaret shared her kindness and love with everyone, this delicious treat will bring warmth and joy to your table.

Saint Margaret of Scotland, pray for us!

Petite Scottish Scones

Ingredients (MAKES 12)

2 cups all-purpose flour
1/3 cup sugar
1 tablespoon baking powder
1/4 teaspoon salt
1/2 cup cold butter
1 large egg
1 cup plus 2 tablespoons heavy cream
1 cup fresh blueberries
1 teaspoon vanilla extract

Tools Checklist

Large bowl
Measuring cups and Measuring spoons
Mixing spoons
Box grater or pastry cutter
Knife
Baking sheet
Pastry brush
Oven mitts
Wire cooling rack

Instructions

1. Preheat the oven to 400°F.
2. In a large mixing bowl, stir together flour, sugar, baking powder, and salt.
3. Grate the butter with the large holes of a box grater and stir it into the flour mixture, or cut the butter into small pieces and use a pastry cutter to cut it into the flour mixture until it resembles coarse meal or sand.
4. Add the egg, 1 cup of cream, blueberries, and vanilla extract (or other mix-ins, listed below) to the flour mixture, stirring until the dough just comes together.
5. Turn the dough out onto a clean countertop and form it into a ball. Press the dough into two 5-inch discs. Use a butter knife to cut each disc into 6 equal wedges.
6. Place the cut scones on an ungreased baking sheet and brush the tops with 2 tablespoons of heavy cream.
7. Bake for about 18 to 20 minutes, until the tops are nicely browned.
8. Allow the scones to cool slightly on a wire rack, then serve them warm.

Note: Other ingredients can be used in the basic scone recipe to create different flavors.

See page 42 for Mix-In options.

Mix-in options:

- Chocolate Chip Scones: Replace the blueberries with 1 cup mini chocolate chips.
- Cranberry-Orange Scones: Replace the blueberries with ¾ cup dried cranberries and 2 tablespoons orange zest.
- Pumpkin Scones: Omit the blueberries and replace half of the heavy cream with ½ cup pumpkin puree and 2 teaspoons pumpkin pie spice.
- Lemon Scones: Omit the blueberries and replace ¼ cup of the heavy cream with ¼ cup lemon juice and 2 tablespoons lemon zest.
- Cinnamon Scones: Omit the blueberries, use brown sugar instead of white sugar, and add 1 to 2 teaspoons ground cinnamon.

Just as Margaret shared her kindness and love with everyone, this delicious treat will bring warmth and joy to your table.

Baked Goods

"Who will teach me
what is most pleasing to God,
that I may do it?"

Saint Kateri Tekakwitha

Saint Lucy

The Shining Light

283–304 * Feast day: December 13

Patron of the blind and those with eye problems

Born in Syracuse, a coastal town of Sicily, Lucy was known for her deep faith, kindness, and courage from a young age. Even though being a Christian was dangerous in her time, Lucy dedicated her life to God as a young girl, promising to stay pure and never marry.

One of the most famous stories about Lucy is her incredible bravery. When a powerful man wanted to marry her, she refused because she had promised herself to God. This made the man very angry, and he reported her to the Roman authorities for being a Christian. Lucy was arrested, but she never lost her faith.

Lucy's name means "light," and she truly brought light to others. Even in the darkest times, her faith shone brightly. One legend says that Lucy lost her sight when she was imprisoned, but God restored her ability to see, making her a symbol of spiritual vision and inner light.

Another story tells how Lucy would secretly bring food to Christians hiding in the catacombs, or underground tunnels. To light her way, she wore a wreath of candles on her head, keeping her hands free to carry as much food as possible. Her selflessness and bravery helped many people during difficult times.

Saint Lucy's feast day is celebrated on December 13, during Advent, a time when we prepare for Christmas. In many countries, especially in Scandinavia, girls dress as Lucy, wearing white dresses with red sashes and wreaths of candles on their heads, bringing light and treats to their families.

One special tradition is baking St. Lucia's Braided Bread. Its beautiful braided shape reminds us of Lucy's candle crown and the way she lit the darkness with hope and love. Sharing this sweet, golden bread with others is a way to honor her spirit of giving, kindness, and bringing God's light to the world.

Saint Lucy, pray for us!

Saint Lucia's Braided Bread

Ingredients

(SERVES 12)

For the dough:

1½ cups milk

1 (.25-ounce) package active dry yeast (2¼ teaspoons)

¼ cup plus 1 tablespoon sugar

6 tablespoons butter, cut into pieces

2 large eggs

¼ cup orange juice

1 tablespoon finely grated orange rind

1 teaspoon salt

5½ cups all-purpose flour

For the glaze and garnish:

2½ cups confectioners' sugar

2½ to 3½ tablespoons orange juice

1/3 cup dried cranberries

Tools Checklist

Measuring cups and Measuring spoons

Knife

Small saucepan

Medium and large bowls

Whisk

Mixing spoons

Plastic wrap

Rolling pin

Baking sheet

Oven mitts

Wire cooling rack

Instructions

For the dough:

1. Warm the milk in a small saucepan, then pour ½ cup of the milk into a large bowl.
2. Add the yeast and 1 tablespoon of sugar to the large bowl with milk and let it set for 5 minutes. Meanwhile, melt the butter in the remaining milk in the saucepan.
3. Add the butter and milk mixture to the yeast mixture. Whisk in the eggs, juice, ¼ cup of sugar, orange rind, and salt.
4. Stir in the flour, 1 cup at a time, until the dough can be gathered into a ball. Knead the dough on a floured surface for 10 minutes, adding more flour until the dough is smooth and elastic and does not stick to your hands.

Instructions continued on next page.

5. Transfer the dough to an oiled bowl, turning it once to coat it. Loosely cover the bowl with plastic wrap and let it rise until it has doubled in size, about 1½ hours.
6. Punch down the dough and divide it into 3 equal parts. Roll each part into a 30-inch-long rope, then braid the ropes together.
7. Transfer the braid to a greased baking sheet. Bring the ends together and pinch them to form a circle. Let the dough rise until it has again doubled in size, about 45 minutes.
8. Preheat the oven to 375°F.
9. Bake the bread for 25 minutes or until golden brown, then let it cool on a wire rack.

For the glaze and garnish:

1. Stir together the confectioners' sugar and orange juice in a medium bowl until smooth.
2. Drizzle the glaze over the cooled bread, then garnish with cranberries.

Sharing this sweet, golden bread with others is a way to honor St. Lucy's spirit of giving, kindness, and bringing God's light to the world.

Saint Dorothy

Flowers from Heaven

Late 3rd century–311 * Feast day: February 6

Patron of brewers, brides, florists, midwives, and newlyweds

Imagine living in a time and place when standing up for what you believe in could be dangerous. That's the world Dorothy lived in. In her town of Caesarea, in the region of Cappadocia (in modern-day Turkey), she was a brave and loving girl known for her kindness and deep faith in God. She spent her days helping others and praying, her heart always full of love and hope.

One day, trouble came when Dorothy was arrested for being a Christian. Officials tried to make her give up her faith, but Dorothy stood firm and proclaimed her love for Jesus Christ.

Legends say, before Dorothy died, a man named Theophilus made fun of her. He mockingly asked her to send him fruits and flowers from heaven's garden. With a smile, Dorothy promised to do so. While she prayed before her death, a child appeared, carrying a gold basket of roses and apples. Dorothy asked the child to take the basket to Theophilus. When he received the miraculous gift, he was so amazed that he became a Christian right then and there.

Saint Dorothy is often shown with a basket of flowers and fruits, reminding us of the beautiful story of her faith. Her story is a wonderful reminder that even in tough times, our faith can inspire and change the hearts of others.

This Flower Bouquet Focaccia is inspired by St. Dorothy's heavenly basket. By arranging colorful vegetables and herbs into beautiful garden designs on top of the bread, we remember the gift of faith that blooms, even in hard times. As we bake and share this bread, we celebrate the beauty, hope, and love that Saint Dorothy showed to the world.

Saint Dorothy, pray for us!

Saint Dorothy

Flower Bouquet Focaccia

Tools Checklist

Measuring cups
Measuring spoons
Large bowl
Plastic wrap (or other bowl cover)
Whisk
Rubber spatula
9 × 13-inch baking dish
Parchment paper
Pastry brush
Knives
Oven mitts

Ingredients

(MAKES ONE 9 X 13-INCH FOCACCIA)

4 cups all-purpose flour or bread flour
2 teaspoons kosher salt
2 teaspoons instant yeast
2 cups lukewarm water
4 tablespoons olive oil, divided
Flaky sea salt
Assorted toppings; suggestions include:

Red onions, thinly sliced, to make flowers
Mini bell peppers, sliced into rounds or strips, to make flowers or individual petals
Chives, to make flower stems
Green onions, to make flower stems or grass
Parsley, to make leaves
Basil, to make leaves or seaweed
Cherry tomatoes, sliced in half lengthwise, to make flower centers or seed pods (dry with a paper towel before placing on focaccia)
Olives, to make rocks or flower centers
Capers, to make seed pods
Rosemary, to make small plants
Thyme, to make small plants
Pepperoni, cut into any shape, to make flowers or accents
Sausage, to make flower centers or seed pods
Shredded Parmesan cheese, to make sand or dirt

Instructions continued on next page.

Instructions

1. In a large bowl, whisk together the flour, salt, and instant yeast. Add the water. Using a rubber spatula, mix until the liquid is absorbed and the ingredients form a sticky dough ball.
2. Rub the surface of the dough lightly with 1 tablespoon of olive oil. Cover the bowl with a damp dish towel, a cloth bowl cover, or plastic wrap and let the dough rise at room temperature until doubled, about 1½ to 2 hours.
3. Line a 9 × 13-inch baking dish with parchment paper or grease the dish with butter. Pour 2 tablespoons of oil into the dish. Roll the dough ball in the oil to coat it all over, forming a rough ball. Rub your hands lightly in the oil to coat them, then, using all your fingers, press straight down into the dough to create deep dimples. If necessary, gently stretch the dough as you dimple to allow the dough to fill the baking dish. Let the dough rise until puffy, about 30 minutes.
4. Set a rack in the middle of the oven and preheat to 425°F.
5. Drizzle the rest of the olive oil over the top of the focaccia, then sprinkle it with flaky sea salt. Prepare your toppings by brushing herbs and vegetables with olive oil and cutting the ingredients into needed shapes, such as stems and leaves. Then, get creative and assemble the toppings into a floral scene.
6. Transfer the pan to the oven and bake for 25 to 30 minutes, until the underside is golden and crisp.
7. Remove the pan from the oven and let the focaccia cool for 10 minutes before cutting and serving.

Note: If you are cutting the focaccia in half to make sandwiches, let it cool completely first.

As we bake and share this bread, we celebrate the beauty, hope, and love that Saint Dorothy showed to the world.

Venerable Emil Kapaun

From Wheatfields to Battlefields

1916–1951

Venerable Father Emil Kapaun was a humble priest and a true hero who showed remarkable courage and compassion during some of the darkest times in history. Born in 1916 on a farm in Kansas, Emil Kapaun grew up with a strong faith and a desire to serve others. After becoming a priest, he felt called to become a military chaplain so he could bring comfort and hope to soldiers in need.

During the end of World War II and the Korean War, Father Kapaun's bravery and selflessness as a US Army chaplain shone brightly. He served on the front lines, risking his life to minister to the soldiers under fire. He celebrated Mass on the battlefield, often using the hood of a Jeep as his altar, and he tirelessly cared for the wounded and dying. But his greatest act of heroism came when he was captured by enemy forces and taken to a prisoner-of-war camp.

Even in captivity, Father Kapaun never stopped serving others. He secretly celebrated Mass and lifted the spirits of his fellow prisoners with his unshakable faith. He was known for his kindness, often giving away his own food and blankets to those who were weaker. His strength and hope kept many men alive, and his faith inspired them to keep going, even in the face of unimaginable hardship. Father Kapaun's life reminds us of the power of faith, kindness, and sacrifice. He gave everything he had to help those around him, even when he had little to give. To honor Father Kapaun's legacy, enjoy these Breadbasket Dinner Rolls. Just as Father Kapaun nourished the bodies and souls of his fellow soldiers, these warm, comforting rolls remind us to share what we have and care for those in need.

Venerable Emil Kapaun, pray for us!

Breadbasket Dinner Rolls

Ingredients

(MAKES 15)

Butter or nonstick cooking spray
1 cup warm water
1/3 cup melted butter
¼ cup sugar
2 tablespoons active dry yeast
1 egg, beaten
½ teaspoon salt
3 cups all-purpose flour
1/8 cup milk, room temperature

Tools Checklist

9 x 13-inch baking pan
Measuring cups and Measuring spoons
Large bowl
Mixing spoons
Stand or hand mixer
Parchment paper
Dish towel
Pastry brush
Oven mitts

Instructions

1. Preheat the oven to 400°F. Grease a 9 x 13-inch baking pan with butter or cooking spray.
2. In a large bowl, combine the water, butter, sugar, and yeast. Let sit until the yeast is bubbly, about 5 minutes. Stir the beaten egg and salt into the yeast mixture.
3. Using a stand mixer or mixing by hand, add the flour 1 cup at a time until you have a soft dough that is not sticky. Then, knead by hand for 10 minutes or with a stand mixer for 5 minutes.
4. Divide the dough into 15 equal pieces, then form them into balls. Place the dough balls in the prepared pan, then cover the pan with parchment paper and a kitchen towel.
5. Let the dough rise for 10 minutes in a warm place. (If time allows, continue to let it rise for up to another 30 minutes.)
6. Lightly brush the dough with milk, then bake on the middle rack for 10 to 12 minutes or just until browned.
7. Let the rolls cool for a few minutes in the pan. Serve when they are cool enough to handle.

Saint Elizabeth of Hungary

Princess of the Poor

1207–1231 * Feast day: November 17

Patron of bakers, nursing homes, brides, and the poor

Elizabeth was no ordinary princess. The daughter of the king of Hungary, born into a life of riches and royal splendor, she chose a different path, giving away everything she had to follow Jesus. Her heart reached out to the people in her kingdom who needed help. Elizabeth's husband knew how much she cared for others, and he supported her fully. Together, they helped those affected by diseases and floods. Elizabeth even gave away royal clothing to those in need!

But what Elizabeth is most famous for is her secret bread deliveries. Can you imagine a princess sneaking out to deliver fresh loaves of bread to the poor? That's what Elizabeth did, with a smile on her face and love in her heart.

One day, someone stopped her and asked what was in her basket. Nervously, Elizabeth showed the contents, and to everyone's astonishment, the bread had turned into a beautiful bouquet of roses! It was like a little wink from God, celebrating her kindness (and keeping her secret!).

Elizabeth's life was not very long; she passed away at only twenty-four. But she lived each day to the fullest, helping others and praying with all her heart. Her story teaches us that simple acts of kindness, like baking bread or sharing a smile, can make a big difference in someone's life.

While others admired Elizabeth's glittering crown, her true treasure was the love and compassion she shared with those in need. Her noble heart turned a life of luxury into a legacy of generosity. Even if you're not a princess, you can still make a difference in the world.

Just like St. Elizabeth, you have the power to help others and spread joy. So why not start by sharing a kind word, a helping hand, or a loaf of Humble Sandwich Bread? It's the small acts of love that truly make the world a better place.

Saint Elizabeth of Hungary, pray for us!

Humble Sandwich Bread

Ingredients

(MAKES 2 LOAVES)

2½ cups warm water

2 (.25-ounce) packages or 1 tablespoon active dry yeast

1 tablespoon sugar

6 to 6½ cups all-purpose flour

2 teaspoons salt

¼ cup butter, softened

Tools Checklist

Measuring cups and Measuring spoons

Large bowl

Mixing spoons

Stand mixer with dough hook (optional)

Dish towels

Two 4 x 8-inch loaf pans

Oven mitts

Wire cooling rack

Instructions

1. Pour ½ cup of the warm water into a bowl (preferably that of a stand mixer, if using one) and stir in the yeast and sugar. Let sit for until foamy, about 5 minutes.
2. Add the rest of the water and about half of the flour. Stir until well blended. Add the rest of the flour, salt, and butter and mix with the dough hook of your stand mixer or by hand until well combined.
3. Continue to knead until smooth and elastic. If using a dough hook, run it for about 8 minutes, poking the dough down occasionally, then turn the dough out onto the countertop and knead a few times by hand to make sure it's evenly smooth.
4. Shape the dough into a ball and put it back into the bowl. Cover the bowl with a dish towel and let it sit for 1 to 1½ hours, until it's doubled in size.
5. Butter two 4 x 8-inch loaf pans. Divide the dough into two equal pieces. Punch the dough down and pat each piece into a rectangle that's about 9 x12 inches, or a bit bigger than a standard piece of paper.

Instructions continued on next page.

6. Starting at a short end of one of the pieces of dough, fold it in thirds, like a letter. Place it seam side down in a loaf pan, then tuck the ends in. Repeat with the other piece of dough.
7. Cover the loaf pans with dish towels and leave them for an hour; they should puff right up out of the pan.
8. Preheat the oven to 375°F and set a rack in the middle of the oven.
9. Bake for 30 to 35 minutes, until the loaves are honey brown. Immediately turn the loaves out of their pans and onto a wire rack to cool.
10. Let the loaves cool completely before slicing.

Just like St. Elizabeth, you have the power to help others and spread joy.

Saint Thorlak of Iceland

Shepherd of the Forgotten

1133–1193 * Feast day: December 23

Patron of Iceland and autism

Even as a young boy, Thorlak loved learning about God and helping people. He was known for being kind, wise, and humble. Thorlak's parents, barely able to earn a living as farmers, noticed their son's talents and made sure he received education from a local priest. Others noticed his gifts, too, and Thorlak was ordained as a deacon before the age of fifteen and became a priest at age eighteen!

Thorlak's love for learning about God made him special. Even though he was not a good speaker, he drew people closer to God. He didn't mind his weaknesses and offered them to God, always doing what was right.

Thorlak left Iceland and traveled to France to study more about being a good priest, and then he returned to Iceland and became a bishop. He helped everyone, giving food and clothes to those in need and advising people about how to solve problems fairly.

Thorlak had a deep love of theology. His fellow priests, who valued practical work, sometimes misunderstood him. In Iceland, where survival depended on hard work and good political connections, a life of prayer seemed strange, but Thorlak persisted in his rigid routine of fasting and prayer.

Thorlak loved the Church and encouraged people to pray and do good deeds. He believed that even small acts of kindness could make a big difference. His gentle spirit and strong faith inspired many people to follow his example.

Thorlak strictly followed rules and struggled socially, but he had a unique way of understanding others. He showed great focus and dedication, helping those who felt left out. Saint Thorlak has become an inspiration for those who have autism and can relate to his special traits.

Just as Thorlak's kindness warmed many hearts, this sweet, spiced Jólakaka will bring joy to your table. This Icelandic Christmas cake is a classic treat that is enjoyed all year round.

Saint Thorlak of Iceland, pray for us!

Jólakaka (Icelandic Coffee Cake)

Ingredients

(MAKES 1 LOAF)

Nonstick cooking spray
2/3 cup butter
3/4 cup sugar
3 eggs
2 cups all-purpose flour
2 teaspoons baking powder
2 teaspoons cardamom
½ teaspoon salt
½ cup milk
¾ cup raisins

Tools Checklist

Loaf pan
Measuring cups
Measuring spoons
Large bowl
Mixing spoons
Oven mitts

Instructions

1. Preheat the oven to 325°F. Grease a loaf pan with nonstick cooking spray.
2. Beat the butter and sugar together until light and fluffy.
3. Add the eggs, one at a time, beating until fully mixed in.
4. Add the flour, baking powder, cardamom, salt, milk, and raisins to the mixture. Stir to mix in fully.
5. Pour the batter into a greased loaf pan. Bake for 45 to 55 minutes.
6. Remove the Jólakaka from the oven and allow it to cool completely before cutting.

Saint Kateri Tekakwitha

Lily of the Mohawks

1656–1680 * Feast day: July 14

Patron of ecology and Native Americans

When Kateri was only four years old, smallpox took the lives of her parents and baby brother and left her scarred and with poor eyesight. Her name, Tekakwitha, means "she who bumps into things," because her weak eyes made her clumsy!

In her Mohawk village in what is now northern New York, Kateri was a gentle and loving girl. She was skilled at weaving and making cornhusk dolls. As she grew up, she became fascinated by her mother's Christian faith. French Jesuit missionaries, called "Black Robes" by the Mohawks, came to her village to teach about Jesus. She was so inspired that she asked to be baptized, and she took the name Catherine, or *Kateri* in Mohawk.

Her new faith caused trouble in her village. Her uncle was annoyed, and her refusal to marry a young warrior angered her relatives. They mocked her and gave her the hardest work to do. Despite being mistreated, Kateri remained strong in her faith.

Determined to live her faith freely, Kateri made a daring escape to a Christian Mohawk village nearly 200 miles away! There, she finally felt like she belonged. She spent her days praying, helping others, and making beautiful crafts. Her faith was a beacon of light to those around her.

Kateri's life was short but impactful. She died at the age of twenty-four, and her last words were, "Jesus, Mary, I love you." Witnesses say her scarred face became radiant after her death, a sign of her true beauty and holiness.

Saint Kateri Tekakwitha teaches us about bravery, faith, and kindness. Even when life was hard, she never lost her love for Jesus. She is a wonderful example of how faith can shine brightly, even in difficult times.

This Golden Cornbread honors Kateri's Mohawk heritage, in which corn was a cherished and important part of daily life. As we bake and share it, we can remember her strong faith, her gentle spirit, and the way she brought hope and love to everyone she met.

Saint Kateri Tekakwitha, pray for us!

Golden Cornbread

Ingredients (MAKES 9 TO 12 PIECES)

1 cup fine yellow cornmeal
1 cup all-purpose flour
1 teaspoon baking powder
1/2 teaspoon baking soda
1/8 teaspoon salt
1/2 cup unsalted butter, melted and slightly cooled
1/3 cup light or dark brown sugar, packed
2 tablespoons honey
1 large egg, at room temperature
1 cup buttermilk, at room temperature (see note)

Optional add-ins (stir into batter just before baking):

1 or 2 chopped jalapeño peppers
1 cup blueberries
1/2 cup each dried cranberries and walnuts
1 cup shredded cheddar cheese
1/2 cup crumbled bacon

Tools Checklist

9-inch square baking dish
Measuring cups
Measuring spoons
Large and medium bowls
Whisk
Oven mitts

Instructions

1. Preheat the oven to 400°F. Grease and lightly flour a 9-inch square baking dish.
2. Whisk the cornmeal, flour, baking powder, baking soda, and salt together in a large bowl.
3. In a medium bowl, whisk the melted butter, brown sugar, and honey together until completely smooth and thick. Then, whisk in the egg until combined. Finally, whisk in the buttermilk. Pour the wet ingredients into the dry ingredients and whisk until combined. Avoid over-mixing.
4. Pour the batter into the prepared baking dish. Bake for 20 minutes or until the top is golden brown, the edges are crispy, and the center is cooked through; use a toothpick to test.

Instructions continued on next page.

5. Allow to cool slightly before slicing and serving with butter, honey, jam, or whatever you like.
6. Wrap leftovers tightly and store at room temperature for up to 1 week.

Note: Buttermilk is best for this recipe. If you don't have any, make the following DIY sour milk: Add 2 teaspoons of fresh lemon juice or white vinegar to a liquid measuring cup. Then, add enough whole milk to make 1 cup total. Stir and let sit for 5 minutes before using.

This Golden Cornbread honors Kateri's Mohawk heritage, in which corn was a cherished and important part of daily life.

Saint Bernadette

The Little Girl of Lourdes

1844–1879 * Feast day: April 16

Patron of illness, people ridiculed for their piety, poverty, shepherds, shepherdesses, and Lourdes, France

Bernadette was a little girl who lived in a town in France called Lourdes. Bernadette was very poor and often sick, and she had a deep love for God.

One day, while gathering wood, Bernadette heard a noise near a cave. When she went to investigate, she saw a beautiful lady in white with a blue sash and a rose on each foot. This lovely lady was the Blessed Virgin Mary! Bernadette prayed the rosary with Mary, and then Our Lady asked Bernadette to come back again. She appeared to Bernadette a total of eighteen times! But many people laughed at Bernadette and thought she was making up stories.

Then, something even more amazing happened. Mary asked Bernadette to dig a well at the spot where she had been appearing. When Bernadette did so, a spring of water appeared. People who bathed in this water were often cured of serious illnesses or disabilities. This miracle made many people believe Bernadette.

Lourdes became a famous place for pilgrims from around the world. Millions of visitors still come to Lourdes each year to pray, seek healing, and see the grotto where Mary appeared to Bernadette.

Despite her ongoing sickness and the teasing she faced, Bernadette remained reverent and firm in her faith. She later joined a convent to continue her life of prayer and helping others. Bernadette teaches us about staying strong in our beliefs and trusting in God's plan.

To celebrate St. Bernadette's inspiring life, bake this Rustic French Baguette. Its simple, hearty crust and soft center remind us of the humble French village where she lived and the daily bread that nourished her family. As you share it, think of Bernadette's humility and faith and the healing hope she brought to so many.

Saint Bernadette, pray for us!

Rustic French Baguette

Ingredients

(MAKES 2 LOAVES)

½ cup warm water

1 (.25-ounce) package or 2¼ teaspoons active dry yeast

1½ cups water, room temperature

1½ teaspoons salt

4½ cups bread flour or all-purpose flour

2 tablespoons cornmeal

1 tablespoon milk

Tools Checklist

Measuring cups and Measuring spoons

Large bowls

Mixing spoons

Cutting board

Dish towel

Large baking sheet

Knives

Pastry brush

Oven mitts

Wire cooling rack

Instructions

1. Pour the ½ cup of warm water into a mixing bowl, then sprinkle the yeast on top. Once the yeast dissolves, stir in the water, the salt, and 4 cups of flour.
2. Sprinkle the remaining ½ cup of flour onto a cutting board, then turn the dough out onto it. Knead the dough until all the flour is mixed in.
3. Place the dough in a greased bowl and cover it with a damp towel. Set the bowl aside in a warm place until the dough doubles in size, about 1 hour.
4. Sprinkle the cornmeal onto a large baking sheet. Punch down the dough, then divide it in half. Shape each half into a 12-inch-long fat rope and place them on the baking sheet.
5. Cut a few ¼-inch-deep diagonal slits in the top of each loaf. Cover the loaves with a damp towel and set them aside to rise for 1 hour.
6. Heat the oven to 400°F. Use a pastry brush to lightly brush the top of each loaf with milk. Bake the bread until it turns golden brown, 20 to 25 minutes.
7. Let the baguettes cool on a rack. Slice and serve once they are cool to the touch.

Chef Notes

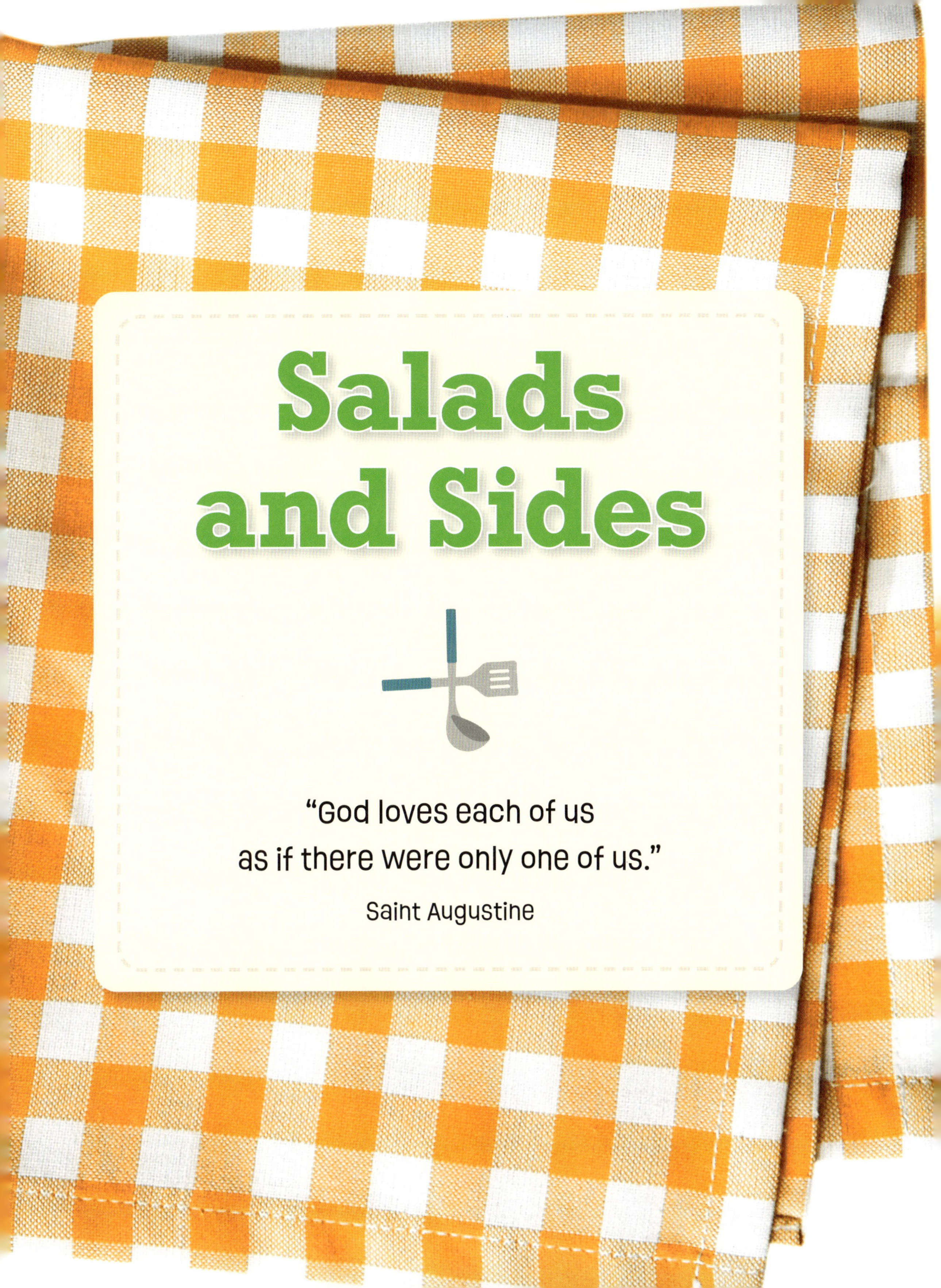

Salads and Sides

"God loves each of us
as if there were only one of us."

Saint Augustine

Saint Brigid of Ireland

The Generous Dairy Maid

451–525 * Feast day: February 1

Patron of Ireland, babies, dairy workers, farmers, sailors, and children without married parents

Around the year 451, a girl named Brigid was born in Ireland. Her mother, a Christian slave baptized by St. Patrick, and her father, a pagan chief, made her life quite unique. Brigid took her mother's faith and put it into action from a young age by helping the poor and the sick. One time, she gave away all of her mother's butter! Later, after Brigid prayed, the butter miraculously reappeared.

At age ten, she was sent to live with her father. Even though she was his slave, she would often take his valuables and give them to the poor. He became so infuriated that he tried to sell her to an Irish king. Being a Christian himself, the king convinced her father to free her from slavery.

Brigid went back to her mother, who was still a slave, running her master's dairy. While staying with her mother, Brigid gave much of the dairy's milk to the poor. God blessed her generosity, making the dairy thrive, and soon her mother was freed from slavery too.

Brigid's father wanted her to marry, but Brigid wished to devote her life to God. She prayed to become so ugly that no one would want to marry her, and God answered her prayer. Later, after Brigid became a nun, she became pretty again.

Brigid's holiness became evident in small ways. One famous story tells of her asking a king for land on which to build a monastery. He refused, so she asked for as much land as her cloak would cover. Miraculously, her cloak expanded to cover many acres. This legend shows how her small acts of love had great power.

Saint Brigid of Ireland found opportunities in everyday life to create holy moments. Celebrate her life by making and sharing this Creamy Mac and Cheese, a nod to her connection to dairy farms and her generous spirit.

Saint Brigid of Ireland, pray for us!

Creamy Mac and Cheese

Ingredients

(SERVES 8)

¼ teaspoon salt
8 ounces elbow macaroni, uncooked
2 tablespoons all-purpose flour
½ teaspoon sea salt
¼ teaspoon garlic powder (optional but recommended)
2 tablespoons salted butter
1 cup whole milk
¼ cup sour cream or Greek yogurt
2 cups shredded cheddar cheese

Tools Checklist

Large pot
Measuring cups and Measuring spoons
Colander/strainer
Small bowl
Mixing spoons
Medium pot
Whisk
Spatula

Instructions

1. Fill a pot with water and ¼ teaspoon salt, then cook the elbow macaroni in the pot according to package instructions. Drain the macaroni and set aside.
2. Mix the flour, sea salt, and garlic powder together in a small bowl.
3. In a medium saucepot over medium heat, melt the butter. Add the flour mixture and whisk to combine.
4. Cook until the mixture is slightly browned, about 1 minute. Add the milk and whisk until the mixture is smooth.
5. Add the sour cream or yogurt and whisk until smooth. Cook on medium-high heat until the mixture is thickened, about 3 to 5 minutes. Do not let it boil.
6. Once the mixture is thick enough to stick to the back of a spatula, reduce the heat to low and add the cheese. Whisk until the cheese is melted and mixture is smooth. Taste and adjust seasoning if desired.
7. Add the cooked pasta to the pot of cheese sauce and stir until the pasta is evenly covered with sauce.
8. Let the mac and cheese cool until the cheese sauce has thickened a bit and sticks to the noodles. Serve warm.

Saints Felicity and Perpetua

Brave Friends of Faith

Unknown–203 / 182–203 * Feast day: March 7

Patrons of mothers, expectant mothers, ranchers, and butchers

Around the year 203, in Carthage (modern-day Tunisia), there lived two brave women named Perpetua and Felicity. Perpetua was a young noblewoman with a baby son, and Felicity was her faithful servant and friend, who was pregnant. Despite the dangers, both women decided to become Christian, which was against the law at that time.

Perpetua's father begged her to give up her faith to save her life, but she believed in Jesus with all her heart and refused. Felicity, who shared Perpetua's strong faith, also refused to abandon God. Both women were arrested and put in a dark, crowded prison.

Even in prison, Perpetua and Felicity found strength in their faith. They prayed together and encouraged other Christians who were imprisoned with them. Perpetua's diary, which she wrote in prison, tells us about their courage and trust in God.

One night, Perpetua had a dream about a golden ladder reaching up to heaven. She saw herself climbing it with Felicity by her side. This dream gave them hope and comfort because they knew God was with them.

Perpetua and Felicity were sentenced to go into the arena with wild animals as punishment for being Christian. They were not afraid, for they knew that Jesus was with them. With courage and joy in their hearts, they became martyrs for their faith.

Saints Perpetua and Felicity remind us to be brave and stand firm in our beliefs, no matter the challenges we face. Their story teaches us about friendship, faith, and courage.

To celebrate the lives of Sts. Perpetua and Felicity, enjoy this Tunisian Market Salad. Like the flavors of this salad, their faith was strong and vibrant, and this colorful dish brings a taste of their homeland to your table. Let their story inspire you to stand firm in your faith and support your friends with love and courage.

Saints Perpetua and Felicity, pray for us!

Tunisian Market Salad

Ingredients

(SERVES 4 TO 6)

2 cups diced cherry tomatoes
1 yellow bell pepper, diced
1 medium red onion, sliced
½ cup sliced black olives
1 medium cucumber, diced
3 tablespoons crumbled feta cheese
3 tablespoons julienne-cut sun-dried tomatoes
3 tablespoons extra-virgin olive oil
1 clove garlic, minced
1 tablespoon lemon juice
Salt and freshly ground black pepper, to taste
1 tablespoon fresh parsley, chopped

Tools Checklist

Knives
Measuring cups
Measuring spoons
Large and small bowls
Whisk

Instructions

1. In a large bowl, toss together the cherry tomatoes, bell pepper, onions, olives, cucumber, feta cheese, and sun-dried tomatoes.
2. In a small bowl, whisk the olive oil, garlic, lemon juice, salt, and pepper.
3. Pour the dressing over the salad mixture and toss to combine. Top with fresh parsley and serve.

Saint Augustine

Seeker of Truth

354–430 * Feast day: August 28

Patron of brewers, printers, and theologians

Do you ever wonder how or why things work? A curious boy named Augustine was born in North Africa in the year 354. He loved reading books and asking questions about everything. Augustine wanted to understand the world and find the real truth.

Augustine's mother, Monica (who also became a saint), was a devoted Christian who prayed for him every day. She wished for him to discover faith in Jesus. However, young Augustine thought his mother's religion was silly. Convinced that his superior intellect would guide him, he left home and ventured to an exciting new life in the city of Rome.

Augustine had an important job in the city, and he lived a life of luxury—but also of sin. One day, he heard a child's voice singing, "Take and read, take and read," and Augustine took this as a sign from God that he should read the Bible. He did, and the passage he read touched his heart deeply. He felt God's love. Augustine chose to change his ways and follow Jesus.

Augustine became a priest and later a bishop. He used his brilliant mind to write many important books about God and the Christian faith. His most famous book, *Confessions*, is like a diary in which he tells the story of his life and how he found God. Augustine's writings have helped many people understand their faith better.

According to legend, God used a small child and a seashell to teach Augustine a valuable lesson. While walking along the beach, Augustine saw a boy using a seashell to try to fill a hole in the sand with all of the water in the ocean! Augustine realized that just as the boy couldn't fit the entire ocean into the hole, humans cannot fully understand the mysteries of God. This taught him humility and wonder in the vastness of our Creator.

Remember this lesson from St. Augustine's life when you enjoy this flavorful Seashell Pasta Salad, filled with veggies. Saint Augustine teaches us to always seek the truth, be humble, and trust in God's love.

Saint Augustine, pray for us!

Saint Augustine

Seashell Pasta Salad

Ingredients

(SERVES 8)

1 (16-ounce) box of pasta shells
½ cup diced red bell pepper
½ cup shredded carrots
½ cup halved cherry tomatoes
¼ cup grated Parmesan cheese
2 tablespoons diced chives
1 cup Italian salad dressing
¼ teaspoon salt
¼ teaspoon ground pepper

Tools Checklist

Medium pot
Knives
Measuring cups
Measuring spoons
Large bowl
Wooden spoon
Lid or other bowl cover

Instructions

1. Prepare the pasta according to the directions on the box.
2. In a large bowl, combine the cooked pasta shells, peppers, carrots, cherry tomatoes, Parmesan, and chives. Mix together with a wooden spoon.
3. Pour the Italian salad dressing over the pasta mixture, then sprinkle it with the salt and pepper. Mix again until all ingredients are evenly coated with the dressing.
4. Cover the bowl and refrigerate the salad until serving time.

Saint Faustina Kowalska

From Potatoes to Roses

1905–1938 * Feast day: October 5

Patron of mercy

Sister Faustina was a humble nun in the Congregation of Sisters of Our Lady of Mercy in Poland during the 1930s. Coming from a poor family and with only three years of basic education, she was given the simplest tasks in the convent, usually in the garden or kitchen.

One of her chores was draining potatoes for the sisters' supper. However, she found her body too weak for the heavy pots, and she often spilled them. Frustrated, Faustina brought the matter to prayer. Jesus responded, "From today on, you will do this easily; I shall strengthen you."

Trusting in Jesus' words, she eagerly approached the job of draining potatoes that evening. Not only did she perform the duty without mishap, she also discovered that the potatoes had been transformed into "whole bunches of red roses, beautiful beyond description." Jesus explained the miracle to her, saying, "I change such hard work of yours into bouquets of beautiful flowers, and their perfume rises up to my throne."

Faustina was chosen by Jesus to spread the message of Divine Mercy. She often had visions of Jesus, who appeared to her as the Divine Mercy, with rays of light shining from his heart. He asked her to have a picture painted of this vision and to share his message of love and mercy with the world.

Faustina kept a diary of her experiences and the messages she received from Jesus. This diary, known as *Divine Mercy in My Soul*, has inspired millions of people to trust in God's mercy and love.

Faustina's life teaches us about the power of faith in overcoming challenges, the importance of trusting in God, and the incredible love and mercy that Jesus has for each of us. As you enjoy these Au Gratin Potatoes, remember that if we offer Jesus willing hands and hearts, our hard work will be pleasing to him, and he will turn our "potatoes into roses."

Saint Faustina Kowalska, pray for us!

Au Gratin Potatoes

Ingredients

(SERVES 6)

Butter, for greasing
4 medium russet potatoes, thinly sliced
½ teaspoon salt, plus more to taste
Ground black pepper, to taste
1 medium onion, sliced into rings
3 tablespoons butter
3 tablespoons all-purpose flour
2 cups milk
1½ cups shredded cheddar cheese

Tools Checklist

1-quart casserole dish
Knives
Measuring cups
Measuring spoons
Medium saucepan
Whisk
Mixing spoons
Aluminum foil
Oven mitts

Instructions

1. Preheat the oven to 400°F. Butter a 1-quart casserole dish.
2. Layer half of the potatoes in the bottom of the prepared casserole dish, then season them with salt and pepper. Layer the onion slices on top of the potatoes, then top them with the remaining potatoes. Season again with salt and pepper.
3. Melt the butter in a medium saucepan over medium heat. Gradually whisk in the flour and ½ teaspoon salt and cook, whisking constantly until the raw flour flavor has cooked off, about 1 minute. Gradually add the milk, about ¼ cup at a time, whisking well each time you add more; adding the milk gradually and whisking it will help prevent lumps in your sauce.
4. Cook the milk mixture, whisking constantly, until it has thickened, about 3 to 5 minutes. Stir in the cheese all at once and continue stirring until it has melted, about 30 to 60 seconds.
5. Pour the cheese sauce over the potatoes and cover the dish with aluminum foil. Bake in the oven until the potatoes are tender and the sauce is bubbly, about 1½ hours.
6. Remove the dish from the oven and wait a few minutes before serving to allow it to set slightly.

Saint Bartholomew

The Brave Apostle

First century * Feast day: August 24

Patron of tanners, plasterers, tailors, leatherworkers, bookbinders, farmers, house painters, butchers, and glove makers

Bartholomew was one of the Twelve Apostles of Jesus and was known for his strong faith and courage. He was from Cana in Galilee and was a close friend of Philip, another apostle. When Philip told him about Jesus, Bartholomew was curious but skeptical at first. However, when he met Jesus, he became a faithful follower.

Bartholomew witnessed many miracles and teachings of Jesus. After Jesus' resurrection and ascension, Bartholomew, like the other apostles, traveled far and wide to spread the Good News. He preached in various countries, sharing the love and message of Jesus with everyone he met. It is said that he even traveled as far as India and Armenia, bringing many people to the faith.

Bartholomew's dedication to spreading Christianity was not without challenges. He faced many dangers, but his faith never wavered. According to tradition, he was martyred for his faith, showing his unwavering commitment to Jesus.

Saint Bartholomew's feast day is celebrated at the end of summer, on August 24, when the last watermelons are ripe and sweet. This connection made St. Bartholomew the unofficial, and accidental, patron saint of this delicious fruit! On the Tiber Island in Rome, a tradition began at the cathedral dedicated to St. Bartholomew, called San Bartolomeo all'Isola. Villagers would attend Mass and then celebrate the great saint with a watermelon festival and market. Games, races, and, of course, plenty of watermelon made the celebration a fitting tribute to St. Bartholomew and the end of summer.

Saint Bartholomew's life teaches us about the importance of faith, courage, and spreading the message of Jesus, no matter the obstacles we face. To honor St. Bartholomew's life, enjoy this refreshing Watermelon and Herb Salad, which reminds us how Bartholomew's faith brought refreshment and sweetness to many.

Saint Bartholomew, pray for us!

Watermelon and Herb Salad

Ingredients

(SERVES 8)

¼ cup basil leaves
¼ cup mint leaves
4 cups cubed watermelon (½-inch cubes)
2 teaspoons lime juice
Kosher salt, or to taste
Chili powder, or to taste
Cracked black pepper, to taste

Tools Checklist

Measuring cups
Measuring spoons
Knife
Large and small bowls
Mixing spoons

Instructions

1. Stack the basil and mint leaves on top of each other and roll tightly into a log. Slice the log lengthwise into thin ribbons.
2. Combine the herbs and watermelon in a large bowl, then drizzle the lime juice on top.
3. Mix the salt and chili powder together, then sprinkle over the watermelon mixture and toss to combine. Add cracked black pepper. Taste and adjust seasonings if needed.
4. Refrigerate the salad for at least 30 minutes before serving.

Saint Helena

The Queen and the True Cross

Around 248–330 * Feast day: August 18

Patron of difficult marriages, divorced people, converts, and archaeologists

Helena was a wise empress who loved God with all her heart. She and her son, Emperor Constantine (who also became a saint), helped Christianity grow and spread through the Roman Empire after Christians had been persecuted there for a long time.

One of the most amazing stories about Helena is how she found the True Cross, the very cross on which Jesus was crucified! At eighty years old, Helena went to Jerusalem to find the cross. She prayed and searched for days, and one day she noticed a sweet-smelling plant (that we now know as basil) growing on a hillside. She asked her helpers to dig there, and they found three crosses.

To figure out which one was the True Cross, a very sick woman was brought to the site of the crosses. She touched each of the three crosses and was immediately healed by touching one of them. Helena knew she had found the right cross.

The cross of Christ was elevated and celebrated, and Christians flocked to venerate it. This event is commemorated each year with the Feast of the Exaltation of the Holy Cross. Helena sent pieces of the True Cross back to Rome and Constantinople and built a large church on the site of Jesus' crucifixion, burial, and resurrection, known today as the Church of the Holy Sepulchre.

Many relics believed to be found by Helena are in Cyprus. With pieces of the True Cross are pieces of Jesus' tunic and the rope that tied Jesus to the cross. Helena built more than eighty churches, including the Church of the Nativity in Bethlehem, the Pater Noster Church on the Mount of Olives, and the Basilica of the Agony in the Garden of Gethsemane. Without her work, the memory of these sacred sites might have been lost forever.

Saint Helena had true love for Jesus and his Cross. Her life teaches us about faith, determination, and kindness. As you make this Holy Pesto and enjoy it as a sauce, topping, or spread, let the fragrant basil remind you of her journey to find the True Cross.

Saint Helena, pray for us!

Holy Pesto

Ingredients (MAKES ABOUT 1½ CUPS)

1/3 cup walnuts
2 large garlic cloves, roughly chopped
2 cups fresh basil leaves, packed
1/2 teaspoon salt
1/4 teaspoon ground black pepper
2/3 cup extra-virgin olive oil
1/2 cup grated Parmigiano-Reggiano cheese

Tools Checklist

Knife
Measuring cups
Measuring spoons
Food processor
Jar or plastic container with lid

Instructions

1. Place the walnuts and garlic in the bowl of a food processor fitted with a steel blade. Process until coarsely chopped, about 10 seconds. Add the basil leaves, salt, and pepper and process until the mixture resembles a paste, about 1 minute.
2. With the food processor running, slowly pour the olive oil through the feed tube and process until the pesto is thoroughly blended. Add the Parmigiano-Reggiano and process for 1 minute more.
3. Store in the refrigerator in a tightly sealed jar or airtight plastic container for up to a week.

Note: Pesto will keep for up to 6 months in the freezer. One idea is to spoon the prepared pesto into the compartments of an ice cube tray and freeze. Then, remove the frozen pesto cubes from the tray and put them in a sealable plastic bag or airtight container.

Saint Anthony of Saint Ann Galvão

The Miracle Worker of Brazil

1739–1822 * Feast day: May 11

Patron of Brazil and expectant mothers

Anthony Galvão was born in 1739 in São Paulo, Brazil, to wealthy and devout Catholic parents who deeply instilled the faith in their ten children. From a young age, Anthony felt called to serve God. As a teenager, he joined the Franciscan Order and became known as Frei Galvão. His family's devotion to St. Ann led him to take the name Anthony of St. Ann. He vowed to defend the Virgin Mary's title of the Immaculate Conception, even to death. He spent his life praying, helping others, and living humbly.

Frei Galvão became famous for his "pills." He wrote a special prayer in Latin on tiny pieces of paper, rolled them into the size of a pill, and gave them to people who were sick or in trouble. Miraculously, many who swallowed these pills were healed.

One amazing example is a woman who had kidney stones. She visited Frei Galvão and swallowed one of his pills, and her pain stopped immediately. Frei Galvão worked closely with the Recollect Sisters of São Paulo as their confessor and established a new convent for them, and he taught the sisters how to make his pills. Today, these pills are still made on rice paper and given out, free of charge, to people every day. Miracles and healings are still reported from taking the pills and praying to the saint.

Frei Galvão was a man of deep prayer; people even said they saw him levitate while praying. Frei Galvão faced many challenges, but he always trusted God. Even when the government forced the convent to close, he stayed calm and listened for what God wanted him to do. He and the sisters waited faithfully, and the convent was reopened. Frei Galvão's life teaches us about the power of faith, helping others, and the miracles that can happen when we trust in God.

To honor St. Anthony of St. Ann Galvão's life, enjoy this Brazilian Vinaigrette Salsa. This bright, flavorful mix of vegetables pairs perfectly with grilled meats, chicken, or fish; in fact, it's often served with *churrasco* (Brazilian-style grilled meats). You can even serve it over rice or with tortilla chips. However you enjoy the salsa, it will bring a taste of Frei Galvão's home to your table.

Saint Anthony of St. Ann Galvão, pray for us!

Brazilian Vinaigrette Salsa

Ingredients

(SERVES 8)

1 large onion, diced

4 tomatoes, diced

1 green or red bell pepper, diced (optional)

1/3 cup chopped parsley

¼ cup white wine vinegar

½ cup olive oil

Salt and pepper, to taste

Tools Checklist

Knives

Measuring cups

Large bowl

Mixing spoons

Instructions

1. Add all ingredients to a bowl and toss to combine.
2. Chill for at least an hour before using.

Note: Keep in mind that flavors, including salt, intensify after sitting, so taste the salsa before serving—you can always add salt if needed. You may also add more vinegar if you prefer a tangier taste.

Saints Louis and Zélie Martin

A Family of Saints

1823–1894 / 1831–1877 * Feast day: July 12

Patrons of illness, mental illness, marriage, parenting, and widowers

Louis Martin dreamed of becoming a priest but was rejected for not knowing Latin. He was disappointed, but he became a skilled watchmaker and faithfully served God and his neighbors. Zélie Guérin longed to be a nun, but poor health prevented her from joining a convent. Instead, she learned to make lace and started her own business.

One day, Louis and Zélie passed each other on a bridge in their French town, Alençon, and everything changed. Zélie heard a voice inside her say, "This is he whom I have been preparing for you." They became acquainted and married a few months later.

The Martins had nine children but faced great heartache, as four of them died young. Despite this, their home was filled with love and laughter, and they extended their goodwill to the needy and even to enemy soldiers during the Franco-Prussian War.

Zélie's lace-making business was so successful that Louis sold his watchmaking business to help her. Their hard work was driven by their desire to serve God. They always found time for prayer and helping others. The secret to their unfailing love was their boundless faith in God. Louis and Zélie taught their children to love and trust in Jesus.

Zélie became very ill and died when their youngest daughter, Thérèse (shown in illustration)—who would become St. Thérèse of Lisieux, the beloved "Little Flower"—was only four years old. The family was heartbroken, but Louis lovingly raised his five daughters and supported them as each joined the convent. As they grew older, Louis's health failed as well, and he eagerly anticipated the day they would all be reunited in heaven.

The Martins are the first married couple to be canonized together, showing us that marriage and family life can be a path to holiness. To celebrate Sts. Louis and Zélie Martin, enjoy this delicious French Grated Carrot Salad. When ordinary ingredients come together, the result can be joyful!

Saints Louis and Zélie Martin, pray for us!

French Grated Carrot Salad

Ingredients

(SERVES 8)

1 pound carrots

1 cup raisins

Zest and juice of 1 lemon

¼ cup orange juice

1 teaspoon Dijon mustard

1 tablespoon white wine vinegar or apple cider vinegar

2 tablespoons olive oil

½ teaspoon salt

Freshly ground black pepper, to taste

2 tablespoons pure maple syrup

½ cup pecans

Tools Checklist

Measuring cups

Measuring spoons

Zester or small grater

Food processor, box grater, or vegetable peeler

Large and small bowls

Whisk

Mixing spoons

Instructions

1. Use a food processor or box grater to grate the carrots or use a vegetable peeler to make ribbons. Place the carrots in a bowl and add the raisins.
2. In a small bowl, whisk together the lemon zest and juice, orange juice, mustard, vinegar, olive oil, salt, pepper, and maple syrup until smooth. Pour the mixture over the carrots and raisins. Sprinkle with the chopped pecans, then toss to combine.
3. Serve cold. For the best flavor, let it sit overnight in the refrigerator.

Chef Notes

Light Lunches

"Remember that God loves you very much."

Saint Padre Pio

Saint Isidore the Farmer

The Faithful Plowman

1070–1130 * Feast day: May 15

Patron of farmers and rural communities

Isidore grew up in a humble family and worked his entire life as a farmer for a wealthy Spanish landowner near Madrid. Even though he didn't have much, Isidore had a big heart and a deep faith in God. He was known for his kindness, generosity, and hard work.

Isidore had three great loves: God, his family, and the soil. No matter how busy he was, he never missed a day of Mass. While working in the fields, he prayed constantly.

One amazing story about Isidore is how angels would help him with his work. People said that while Isidore was praying, angels would take up the plow and finish his tasks for him. This miraculous help allowed Isidore to do the work of several men, and the fields he worked on always produced abundant crops.

Isidore and his wife, Maria, who is also a saint, showed their neighbors that poverty, hard work, and difficult times cannot destroy happiness if accepted with faith in Christ. Although they had little, Isidore shared what they had, especially his meals, even if it meant he would go without food. He often brought the hungry to his home, where Maria was always ready with a pot of stew.

One day, Isidore brought so many people home that they ran out of food. When Maria told Isidore the pot was empty, he insisted she look again. Like the miracle of the loaves and fishes, there was more stew in the pot, and Maria was able to feed everyone!

Saint Isidore's life teaches us about the importance of faith, hard work, and kindness. To honor his dedication to farming and love of the land, enjoy this refreshing Spanish Gazpacho. This delicious gazpacho brings a taste of Spain's bountiful harvest to your table.

Saint Isidore the Farmer, pray for us!

Spanish Gazpacho

Instructions

1. Combine all ingredients in a blender and blend until smooth.
2. Chill in the refrigerator for at least an hour before serving.
3. If desired, top individual servings with fresh chopped vegetables, croutons, or crusty bread.

Ingredients (SERVES 6)

2 pounds ripe Roma tomatoes, halved, with core and seeds removed

1 small cucumber, peeled and with seeds removed

1 medium green bell pepper, cored

½ small red onion, peeled

2 small garlic cloves (or 1 large clove), peeled

3 tablespoons olive oil

2 tablespoons sherry vinegar

1 teaspoon salt

½ teaspoon freshly cracked black pepper

½ teaspoon ground cumin

Tools Checklist

Knives

Vegetable peeler

Measuring spoons

Blender

Saint Michael the Archangel

The Mighty Protector

Feast day: September 29

Patron of the military, police officers, firefighters, bankers, grocers, death, and people who work in dangerous conditions

Saint Michael the Archangel is a powerful and mighty protector. He is one of the most famous angels in heaven and is known as the leader of God's army. Michael's name means "who is like God," and he is mentioned several times in the Bible.

Michael is often depicted as a strong warrior, wearing armor and carrying a sword. His most important battle was when he fought the dragon, who represented the devil, and his evil angels. With God's power, Michael and the angels defeated the dragon and threw him out of heaven. This shows us that good always triumphs over evil with God's help.

Saint Michael has many important roles. He is the protector of the Church and all Christians. People often ask for his help and protection in times of danger or when they are struggling with temptation. Michael is also known as the guardian of souls, guiding and defending them as they journey to heaven.

Throughout history, many miracles have been attributed to St. Michael's intercession. He has appeared to people in times of need, offering protection and guidance. Because of his bravery and loyalty, St. Michael is an example of strength, courage, and faith.

Saint Michael shares his feast day, September 29, with the archangels Gabriel and Raphael. To honor St. Michael and his powerful protection, enjoy these "Angeled" Eggs (Avocado Deviled Eggs). Michael is a strong and mighty guardian, and these delicious and healthy eggs bring a burst of flavor and nutrition to your table.

Remember, whenever you face challenges or need protection, you can always ask St. Michael for his help.

Saint Michael the Archangel, pray for us!

"Angeled" Eggs (Avocado Deviled Eggs)

Ingredients

(MAKES 24)

12 large hard-boiled eggs, peeled
1 ripe avocado
½ cup mayonnaise
Zest and juice of 1 lemon
½ teaspoon salt
½ teaspoon freshly ground black pepper
4 slices cooked bacon

Tools Checklist

Knives
Medium bowl
Measuring cups
Measuring spoons
Mixing spoons
Emulsion blender or food processor (optional)

Instructions

1. Slice the hard-boiled eggs in half lengthwise. Remove the yolks and place them in a bowl.
2. Halve the avocado, remove the pit, and scoop the flesh into the bowl with the egg yolks. Add the mayonnaise, lemon zest and juice, salt, and pepper to the bowl. Mix together until smooth, either by hand, with an emulsion blender, or with a food processor.
3. Spoon the avocado and egg-yolk filling into the egg-white halves.
4. Roughly chop the bacon and sprinkle it on top of the eggs.
5. Refrigerate for at least 30 minutes before serving.

Saint Andrew

Fisher of Men

First century * Feast day: November 30
Patron of fishers, singers, golf, Russia, and Scotland

Andrew was one of Jesus' Twelve Apostles and the brother of the Apostle Peter. Born in the small fishing village of Bethsaida, Andrew grew up learning the skills of a fisherman. He loved spending time on the Sea of Galilee, casting nets and catching fish with his family.

One day, while Andrew was fishing, he met Jesus. Andrew was so impressed by Jesus' teachings that he immediately went to find his brother Simon (who was later named Peter by Jesus), telling him, "We have found the Messiah!" From that moment on, the brothers left their fishing boats to follow Jesus and become "fishers of men."

Andrew was known for his strong faith and his willingness to bring others to Jesus. He traveled far and wide to share the Good News, spreading Jesus' message of love and salvation. His missionary journeys took him to many places, including Greece and the land we know now as Russia.

One of the most remarkable stories about St. Andrew is his martyrdom. When he was sentenced to death for preaching about Jesus, he was tied to an X-shaped cross, which is now known as St. Andrew's Cross. Even in his final moments, Andrew continued to share his faith, inspiring many people to follow Jesus.

Like St. Andrew, we are called to spread the love of God and be shining examples of his goodness in the world. Enjoy this delicious Smoked Salmon Spread in honor of the fishers of men. Serve it with crackers or bread and share it with your family and friends, remembering St. Andrew's dedication and love for Jesus.

Saint Andrew, pray for us!

Smoked Salmon Spread

Ingredients

(SERVES 8)

8 ounces cream cheese, softened
2 tablespoons sour cream
1 teaspoon dried dill
½ teaspoon black pepper
½ teaspoon garlic powder
2 teaspoons lemon juice
2 teaspoons Worcestershire sauce
8 ounces smoked salmon

Tools Checklist

Meauring spoons
Medium bowl
Mixing spoons
Knife
Rubber spatula

Instructions

1. Add the cream cheese, sour cream, dill, black pepper, garlic powder, lemon juice, and Worcestershire sauce to a medium mixing bowl and whip until well blended and creamy.
2. Cut or tear the smoked salmon into small pieces, then fold the salmon into the cream cheese mixture with a rubber spatula.
3. Refrigerate the dip for at least one hour prior to serving to allow the flavors to develop.
4. Serve with vegetables, crackers, bagels, or pieces of bread.

Saint Rose of Lima

The Flower of Peru

1586–1617 * Feast day: August 23

Patron of embroiderers, gardeners, florists, people who are harassed for their piety, those suffering family problems, the Americas, Peru, India, and the Philippines

Even as a baby, Isabel de Flores was so enchanting that she was called "Rose," the most beautiful of all flowers. Growing up in Lima, Peru, Rose showed a deep love for God and a desire to live a holy life from a young age.

As Rose grew into a young woman, her beauty caught the attention of many young men, who saw her as the perfect future wife. However, Rose had no interest in marriage and wanted to become a nun. Concerned that her beauty was a distraction, she cut off her hair and rubbed pepper on her face and lime juice on her hands to make herself look unattractive.

Rose joined the Third Order of St. Dominic as a lay member and spent her days praying, fasting and performing self-imposed penances. Disguised under roses, she wore a heavy silver crown with spikes to remind herself of Jesus' crown of thorns.

Rose later moved into a hut in her family's garden. She earned money by selling her flowers during the day and doing needlework at night, making designs with colorful threads on cloth. With the money she earned, Rose helped her family and bought food for the needy people in her community. With help from her brother, she added rooms to her hut where she cared for homeless children and the elderly. Her kindness and compassion made her a much-loved woman throughout her country.

To celebrate St. Rose's love for her homeland, enjoy this delicious Peruvian Solterito. This traditional salad, made with fresh vegetables and herbs, is a perfect way to honor the beautiful garden of St. Rose's heart. Rose's life teaches us to use our talents to bring others closer to Christ.

Saint Rose of Lima, pray for us!

Peruvian Solterito

Ingredients

(SERVES 6)

For the dressing:

3 tablespoons fresh lemon juice or red wine vinegar
6 tablespoons olive oil
2 tablespoons chopped fresh mint
2 tablespoons chopped fresh cilantro
3 garlic cloves, minced
¼ teaspoon salt
¼ teaspoon freshly ground black pepper

For the salad:

¾ cup thinly sliced red onion (see note)
½ cup thinly sliced radishes
½ cup cherry tomatoes, sliced in half
1 can of lima beans, drained and rinsed
1 can of corn or white hominy, drained
¼ cup crumbled feta or goat cheese
½ cup chopped red bell pepper (or jalapeno pepper, for more spice)
¼ cup black olives, sliced (optional)

Tools Checklist

Knives
Measuring spoons
Measuring cups
Large and small bowls
Whisk or immersion blender
Mixing spoons

Instructions

For the dressing:

1. Place all ingredients in a small bowl. Use a whisk or immersion blender to mix the ingredients together.

For the salad:

1. Place all of the ingredients in a large bowl.
2. Add the salad dressing and stir to combine.
3. Cover and chill in the refrigerator for at least 30 minutes before serving.

Note: To cut the harsh flavor of raw onion, soak the onion slices in ice water for 10 minutes. Drain before adding to the salad.

Saint Padre Pio

The Saint With Healing Hands

1887–1968 * Feast day: September 23

Patron of adolescents and civil defense volunteers; invoked by those in need of stress relief and spiritual healing

From a young age, Francesco Forgione had amazing abilities. He could see guardian angels and speak with Jesus and Mary! It came so naturally to him that he thought everyone else could do it too. Born in a small Italian village in 1887, he grew up attending daily Mass with his family and serving as an altar boy. His deep faith and strong desire to serve God led him to join the Capuchin Franciscan Friars at just fifteen years old, where he took the name Pio and came to be called Padre Pio.

One day, while praying, Padre Pio received the stigmata—the wounds of Christ—on his hands, feet, and side. These painful wounds never became infected and stayed with him for 50 years, drawing many people to him for inspiration and healing.

Padre Pio's hands were special not only because of the stigmata but also because of the good works he performed. He used his hands to bless, heal, and comfort people. He spent long hours listening to confessions and giving advice, helping countless people find peace and faith.

Padre Pio could read people's hearts, knowing what they were thinking and feeling, which helped him provide better guidance during confession. He also had the gift of bilocation, meaning he could be in two places at once!

Despite these extraordinary gifts, Padre Pio remained humble and dedicated his life to serving others. People from all over the world came to see him, and many experienced miracles through his prayers. His deep love for God and others made him a beloved figure. He often said, "Pray, hope, and don't worry. Worry is useless. God is merciful and will hear your prayer."

To celebrate St. Padre Pio's life and the amazing work of his healing and helping hands, enjoy these Ham and Cheese Hand Pies. These delicious hand pies remind us of the care and love our own hands can share with others.

Saint Padre Pio, pray for us!

Ham and Cheese Hand Pies

Ingredients

(MAKES 12)

1/3 cup whole grain mustard
3 tablespoons honey
1 large egg
Salt, to taste
1 tablespoon water
1 (17.3-ounce) package frozen puff pastry, thawed
1 (8-ounce) package sliced Swiss cheese, torn into bite-sized pieces
6 slices deli ham, torn into bite-sized pieces
Freshly ground black pepper
Sesame seeds, for sprinkling

Tools Checklist

Measuring cups
Measuring spoons
Medium and small bowls
Mixing spoons
Rolling pin
Knife
Pastry brush
Fork
Parchment paper
2 baking pans
Oven mitts

Instructions

1. Preheat the oven to 375°F.
2. Add the mustard and honey to a medium bowl and stir to combine.
3. Beat the egg with a pinch of salt and 1 tablespoon water in a small bowl to make an egg wash, then set aside.
4. Unfold the 2 sheets of puff pastry onto a lightly floured surface. Arrange them next to each other, so they overlap slightly on a long side, and gently press them together to make 1 large sheet.
5. Roll the pastry out to a 20 x 15-inch rectangle, then use a sharp knife to cut them into 5-inch squares, for a total of 12 squares.
6. Spread about 1 teaspoon of honey mustard on one half of each pastry square, leaving a little space around the edges. Add some cheese and ham on top of the honey mustard.

Instructions continued on next page.

7. Brush the edges with the egg wash. Fold each square over the filling to make a triangle. Press the edges with your fingers to seal them, then gently press the edges again with a fork to make sure they stay closed.
8. Divide the folded hand pies among 2 parchment-lined baking pans, spacing evenly. Brush the tops with egg wash and sprinkle them with pepper and sesame seeds. Chill in the freezer for 30 minutes.
9. Cut a few slits in the top of each hand pie to let steam escape while baking. Bake until golden brown and puffed, about 30 to 35 minutes, rotating the baking pans top to bottom and front to back halfway through.
10. Let cool slightly, then serve with remaining honey mustard on the side for dipping.

To celebrate St. Padre Pio's life and the amazing work of his healing and helping hands, enjoy these Ham and Cheese Hand Pies.

Saint Brendan the Navigator

Faith and Adventure

Around 484–577 * Feast day: May 16

Patron of sailors, mariners, and travelers

Brendan was an Irish monk filled with a humble desire to share the love of Christ and the Church. He set out with a group of fellow monks on a daring journey across the sea, eager to spread the gospel to unknown lands.

The voyage of St. Brendan was filled with incredible, legendary tales. His group encountered sea monsters, talking birds, and islands that were actually giant sea creatures. One famous story claims that Brendan and his monks celebrated Easter on what they thought was an island. But, as they lit a fire to cook their meal, the island began to move—it was a giant whale! Despite these dangers, Brendan's faith never wavered, and he continued his journey.

After seven years of exploring the seas, Brendan returned to Ireland to evangelize and establish monasteries. His stories of adventure and faith inspired many people to trust in God and seek their own journeys. Brendan's life teaches us about courage, faith, and trust in God. His journey reflects our own quest for meaning and belonging in life.

To honor St. Brendan, enjoy these delicious Fish Cakes. Just as Brendan's voyages were filled with the bounty of the sea, this tasty recipe brings a bit of that adventurous spirit to your table.

Saint Brendan the Navigator, pray for us!

Fish Cakes

Ingredients

(MAKES 6)

1 egg

12 ounces (about 1½ filets) cod, cooked and flaked

5 tablespoons Italian-style breadcrumbs

2 tablespoons mayonnaise

1 tablespoon lime juice

¼ teaspoon paprika

¼ celery salt

Dash of pepper

3 teaspoons butter

Tools Checklist

Large bowl

Whisk

Measuring spoons

Spatula

Lid or other bowl cover

Frying pan

Spoon

Instructions

1. Crack the egg into a large bowl and beat it with a whisk.
2. Break up the cod filets into bite-sized pieces and mix with the egg. Then, add the breadcrumbs, mayonnaise, lime juice, paprika, celery salt, and pepper. Mix well with a spatula.
3. Cover the bowl and chill for 15 minutes in the refrigerator.
4. Melt the butter in a frying pan over medium-low heat. When the butter starts to bubble, spoon six equal mounds of the fish mixture into the pan. Press down on them lightly with the back of the spoon to flatten the tops.
5. Cook the fish cakes for 3 to 4 minutes on each side. Serve warm.

Saint Martha

The Busy Helper

First century * Feast day: July 29

Patron of homemakers, cooks, domestic workers, restaurant servers, and hotel employees

Martha was a dear friend of Jesus who loved helping others. She lived in the village of Bethany with her sister, Mary, and brother, Lazarus. Martha was known for her hospitality, always welcoming guests and making sure everyone felt at home.

One of the most familiar stories about Martha is when Jesus visited their home. Martha was busy cooking and cleaning, wanting everything to be perfect for Jesus. Meanwhile, her sister Mary sat at Jesus' feet, listening to his teachings. Frustrated, Martha asked Jesus to tell Mary to help her. But Jesus gently reminded Martha that spending time with him was the most important thing. This taught Martha—and all of us—that while serving others is good, we must also take time to be with God.

Martha's story didn't end there. When Lazarus fell seriously ill, Martha and Mary sent for Jesus. But before he arrived, Lazarus died. Despite her grief, Martha showed great faith. She told Jesus, "I know that even now God will give you whatever you ask." Jesus performed a miracle by raising Lazarus from the dead, showing Martha the power of faith and God's love.

Martha is remembered for her hard work, hospitality, and deep faith. She teaches us that it's important to serve others, but we should spend time listening to Jesus and trusting in God's plan.

Saint Martha's life is a beautiful example of balancing work and faith. To honor St. Martha, enjoy this delicious Crunchy Chicken Salad. This tasty salad is perfect for welcoming family and friends to your table, just as Martha welcomed Jesus into her home. Remember St. Martha's love for service and faith as you share this meal.

Saint Martha, pray for us!

Saint Martha

Crunchy Chicken Salad

Ingredients

(SERVES 6)

¾ cup mayonnaise
½ cup sour cream
1 tablespoon lemon juice
2 boneless, skinless chicken breasts, cooked and cubed
1 cup seedless red grapes, halved
1 whole apple, diced
1 cup thinly sliced celery
1 cup pecan halves, toasted
Salt and pepper, to taste

Tools Checklist

Knives
Measuring cups
Measuring spoons
Large bowl
Mixing spoons

Instructions

1. In a large bowl, mix the mayonnaise, sour cream, and lemon juice until blended.
2. Add the chicken, grapes, apple, celery, and pecans. Toss to coat all ingredients with the mayonnaise mixture. Add salt and pepper to taste.
3. Serve over lettuce or on croissants or bread.

Saint Sebastian

The Brave Soldier

Around 255–288 * Feast day: January 20

Patron of archers, pin-makers, athletes, and a holy death

Sebastian was a courageous soldier in the Roman army and was known for his leadership and dedication. Even though it was dangerous to be a Christian at that time, Sebastian never hid his faith and used his position in the army to help other Christians who were being punished. He would secretly visit them in prison, bringing comfort and encouragement. He also helped many soldiers and their families learn about Jesus and become Christians themselves.

When the Roman Emperor Diocletian discovered Sebastian's faith, he was furious. He ordered the soldiers to tie Sebastian to a tree and shoot him with arrows. Afterward, the soldiers left him for dead, but God had other plans. A kind Christian woman found Sebastian still alive and took him to her home, where she nursed him back to health.

When he was strong enough, Sebastian did not hide away or live a quiet life to avoid being found. Instead, he did what many saints did: he went right back out to proclaim the Gospel. He went back to the emperor to defend his faith. Sadly, this time, Sebastian was martyred for his unfailing belief in Jesus.

Saint Sebastian's story teaches us about courage, faith, and the importance of standing up for what is right, even when it's difficult. To honor St. Sebastian, enjoy these delicious Antipasto Kebabs. Let the bold flavors remind us how he stood strong in his faith, and let's stand strong in ours too.

Saint Sebastian, pray for us!

Saint Sebastian

Antipasto Kebabs

Ingredients

(MAKES 16)

For the dressing:

¼ cup olive oil
1 tablespoon balsamic vinegar
2 teaspoons Dijon mustard
1 teaspoon garlic powder
½ tablespoon Italian seasoning
¼ teaspoon kosher salt

For the skewers:

16 grape tomatoes
16 pieces fresh basil
16 mozzarella balls
8 ounces Genoa salami, thinly sliced
16 black olives, pitted and drained
8 whole pepperoncini, cut in half with stems removed

Tools Checklist

Measuring cups
Measuring spoons
Knives
Medium bowl
Whisk
Food skewers
Pastry brush

Instructions

For the dressing:

1. Whisk together all dressing ingredients in a medium bowl and set aside.

For the skewers:

1. Skewer the ingredients onto a food skewer in whatever order you like. Fold the basil, salami, and pepperoncini in half to make them bite-sized before adding to the skewer.
2. Brush each skewer with the dressing and then serve.

Saint Andrew Dũng-Lạc and Companions

The Heroes of Vietnam

1795–1839 * Feast day: November 24

Patrons of Vietnam

Saint Andrew Dũng-Lạc was a courageous priest from Vietnam who lived in the nineteenth century. Born into a poor family, he discovered Christianity from missionaries and decided to become a priest to share Jesus' message.

Andrew had many friends who loved God and wanted to spread the Christian faith. During this time, Christians in Vietnam were persecuted. The government arrested many believers, hoping to stop the spread of Christianity. Churches were destroyed, and religious instruction was forbidden. Sometimes even Christian families and villages were attacked.

The king of one of the Vietnamese kingdoms banned foreign missionaries and tried to force Vietnamese Catholics to publicly deny their faith. Andrew and his companions refused to give up their faith, even when it meant punishment or suffering. They believed in God's love and stood firm in their beliefs.

Saint Andrew Dũng-Lạc was one of 117 Catholics martyred for the faith in Vietnam in the nineteenth century. Their bravery inspired others to remain faithful to God. These martyrs gave their lives for their Church and their country. Their example showed the importance of spreading the Gospel of Christ and led to more people becoming Catholic in Vietnam. All 117 were canonized together in 1988 by Pope St. John Paul II.

To honor St. Andrew Dũng-Lạc and the Vietnamese martyrs, enjoy these delicious Vietnamese Spring Rolls. Just as these spring rolls are filled with bold and vibrant ingredients, let's fill our lives with bold faith, courage, and love, remembering the people who courageously stood up for the Catholic faith.

Saint Andrew Dũng-Lạc and companions, pray for us!

Vietnamese Spring Rolls

Ingredients (MAKES ABOUT 15)

For the spring rolls:

1 package rice vermicelli noodles

1 large carrot, peeled and shredded or sliced into thin strips

1 large English cucumber, peeled and thinly sliced

1 pound small shrimp, peeled, deveined, and cooked, with tails removed (or 1 pound chicken, cooked and diced)

1 bunch fresh mint leaves

1 bunch fresh basil leaves

1 bunch fresh cilantro

1 (12-ounce) package spring roll wrappers

For the peanut dipping sauce:

3/4 cup sweet chili sauce

1/3 cup peanut butter, smooth or crunchy

1/2 teaspoon low-sodium soy sauce

1/2 teaspoon hoisin sauce

Tools Checklist

Medium pot
Colander/strainer
Vegetable peeler
Knives
Measuring cups
Measuring spoons
Small bowls
Pie pan or similar deep dish
Plate
Whisk

Instructions

For the spring rolls:

1. Cook the vermicelli noodles in boiling water according to the package instructions. Drain and rinse with cold water.
2. Gather the veggies, shrimp, and herbs, placing each ingredient in a separate small bowl or pile on your work surface so they are easy to see and grab what you need when filling the rolls.
3. Add about 1 inch of water to a large, deep dish or pie pan. Place one spring roll wrapper in the water and let it soak for about 10 to 15 seconds. Remove the wrapper (it should still feel rather firm) and place it on the countertop or a plate.

Instructions continued on next page.

4. Layer 1 or 2 pieces of each veggie, a few shrimp, a few leaves of each herb, and a pinch of noodles on the bottom half of the spring roll wrapper.
5. Fold the sides of the spring roll in, covering the ingredients. Then pull the bottom edge up and over the ingredients, sealing everything together tightly, and roll it up like a burrito. Repeat with the remaining wrappers and filling ingredients.
6. Serve with the peanut dipping sauce (see below). Wrap leftover rolls individually in plastic wrap (to keep the wrappers soft and prevent them from sticking together) and store in the fridge in an airtight container for up to 3 days.

For the peanut dipping sauce:

1. Whisk together all sauce ingredients until smooth. Serve on the side for dipping.

Note: Be careful when soaking the wrappers. They will soften as you add the fillings, so if you soak them for too long, they will be too soft and will tear when you roll them up.

Just as these spring rolls are filled with bold and vibrant ingredients, let's fill our lives with bold faith, courage, and love, remembering the people who courageously stood up for the Catholic faith.

Delicious Dinners

"In God's will, there is great peace."

Saint Josephine Bakhita

Saint Lawrence

The Holy Jokester

225–258 * Feast day: August 10

Patron of schoolchildren, the poor, cooks, and comedians

Have you ever met someone who could make you laugh, even in tough times? That was St. Lawrence! Born in the third century, Lawrence was a deacon in Rome who loved helping others and always had a cheerful spirit.

Lawrence worked for Pope Sixtus II, helping the poor and distributing the Church's wealth. One day, the Roman Emperor Valerian demanded that Lawrence turn over all the treasures of the Church. Lawrence asked for three days to gather everything. During that time, he gave away as much of the Church's money as he could to those in need.

When the emperor came to collect the treasures, Lawrence presented him with people—the poor, the sick, and the needy—saying, "These are the true treasures of the Church." The emperor was furious! He ordered Lawrence to be executed.

Even in the face of death, Lawrence kept his sense of humor. Legend says that he kept making jokes right up to the end. His brave and funny words have made people remember him for centuries. His story teaches us about the importance of generosity, courage, and finding joy in difficult, even dangerous, situations.

To celebrate St. Lawrence, let's make some delicious BBQ Rub. Just like Lawrence's humor added spice to his life, this BBQ Rub will add amazing flavor to your grilled dishes. As you enjoy your meal, remember to be kind, brave, and always find a reason to smile, just like St. Lawrence.

Saint Lawrence, pray for us!

Saint Lawrence

BBQ Rub

Ingredients

(MAKES 5 TO 6 OUNCES,
ENOUGH FOR SEVERAL POUNDS OF MEAT)

3 tablespoons brown sugar
1 tablespoon sweet paprika
1 tablespoon smoked paprika
1 tablespoon chili powder
1 tablespoon dry mustard
1 tablespoon ground cumin
1 tablespoon garlic powder
1 tablespoon onion powder
1 tablespoon kosher salt
¼ teaspoon ground black pepper
¼ teaspoon cayenne pepper (optional)

Tools Checklist

Measuring spoons
Small bowl
Mixing spoon
Fork

Instructions

1. Combine all of the ingredients in a small bowl. Stir well to combine, using a fork to break up any clumps.
2. Rub generously on meat, such as chicken, pork, or beef, before grilling or smoking.

Blessed Cyprian Michael Tansi

Africa's Faithful Servant

1903–1964 * Feast day: January 20
Patron of Nigerian priests

Blessed Cyprian Michael Tansi was one of the first native Nigerians to become a priest and serve his own people. He was born in 1903 and named Iwene Tansi. His parents were not Christians, but they sent him to a school run by Catholic missionaries. There, he learned about Jesus and took the name Michael when he was baptized.

At the age of sixteen, Michael became a teacher in the Catholic schools started by the missionaries. His deep faith and desire to serve God then led him to become a priest, despite his parents' anger. Unlike the missionary priests, Father Michael was African-born and had a special connection with his people. He worked tirelessly to help his parishioners, traveling by foot or bicycle from village to village, preaching and setting up prayer centers that later became parishes.

Father Michael poured his energy into improving the well-being of his community. He helped build churches, schools, and homes for older students without families. He was an excellent teacher, critiquing pagan traditions and caring for orphans and young women. His love for God and his community made a big difference in many lives.

Father Michael eventually felt called to spend more time in quiet prayer as a monk. He moved to England and joined the Cistercian Order, taking the name Cyprian. As a monk, he continued to pray for his people and stay connected to his African roots. He hoped to one day start a monastery in Nigeria, and while this did not happen before his death, a monastery was started in nearby Cameroon.

We can celebrate Blessed Cyprian Michael Tansi with an authentic African dish. This One-Pot Jollof Rice with Shrimp is delicious and reminds us of how Father Michael brought together his people, his culture, and the Catholic faith. As you enjoy this flavorful dish, remember the humble monk who dedicated his life to God, spreading the faith, and helping others. Let his example inspire us to live with kindness, humility, and faith.

Blessed Cyprian Michael Tansi, pray for us!

One-Pot Jollof Rice with Shrimp

Ingredients (SERVES 16)

Olive oil
1 bell pepper, diced
1 medium yellow onion, diced
1 cup diced carrots (fresh or frozen)
1 (28-ounce) can diced tomatoes
1 teaspoon thyme
1 teaspoon rosemary
1 teaspoon garlic powder
1 teaspoon smoked paprika
1½ teaspoons salt
1 teaspoon pepper
2 cups chicken or vegetable broth
1 (6-ounce) can tomato paste
1 cup water
1 cup sweet peas (fresh or frozen)
1 pound shrimp, peeled and deveined
2 cups long grain rice, such as basmati, rinsed

Tools Checklist

Large pot
Knives
Measuring cups
Measuring spoons
Mixing spoons

Instructions

1. In a large pot, add just enough olive oil to coat the bottom, then place it over medium heat.
2. Add the vegetables (except the peas), diced tomatoes, seasonings, broth, tomato paste, and water. Cook on low for 10 minutes.
3. After the vegetables have simmered, add the peas, shrimp, and rice. Cook for another 30 minutes, or until the rice is fully cooked and shrimp are pink.
4. Serve hot.

Saint Carlo Acutis

The Digital Disciple

1991–2006 * Feast day: October 12
Patron of the internet

In many ways, Carlo Acutis was just like any other boy—he loved playing soccer, hanging out with friends, playing video games, and eating pizza. But there was something extra-special about Carlo: he had a deep love for Jesus and a natural talent for computers.

Carlo was born in 1991 in London and grew up in Italy. Even as a young child, Carlo went to Mass daily and prayed the rosary. His faith was the most important thing in his life. He believed that the internet could be used to share God's love with others. Carlo taught himself computer programming from an early age and created websites with a spiritual focus, including his widely praised database of miracles from around the world. He wanted everyone to know how amazing the Eucharist is and how much Jesus loves us. Carlo's love for the Eucharist also inspired his parents, relatives, friends, and others to attend daily Mass.

Carlo was also known for his kindness. He would stand up for kids who were bullied and help his friends with their homework. He was always ready to lend a hand to anyone in need. Carlo once said, "All people are born as originals, but many die as photocopies." He encouraged everyone to be their true selves and use their unique gifts for good.

Carlo got very sick with leukemia when he was only fifteen years old. Even though he was in a lot of pain, he offered up his suffering for the Pope and the Church. Carlo died in 2006, but his legacy lives on. He is an inspiration to young people everywhere, showing us that we are all called to be saints!

To honor St. Carlo Acutis, enjoy making this Pronto Pizza Dough. Carlo loved pizza, and this easy dough recipe will help you make delicious homemade pizzas to share with family and friends. As you knead the dough, remember Carlo's love for Jesus and his dedication to using his talents to spread God's love.

Saint Carlo Acutis, pray for us!

Pronto Pizza

Ingredients

(SERVES 8)

1 (.25-ounce) package or 2¼ teaspoons active dry yeast

2 tablespoons honey or 1 tablespoon sugar

1 cup water, heated to 110°F

2½ to 3¼ cups bread flour or all-purpose flour

2 tablespoons olive oil

1 teaspoon salt

Pizza toppings of your choice

Tools Checklist

Pizza stone, pizza pan, or baking sheet

Measuring cups and Measuring spoons

Large bowl

Wooden spoon

Rolling pin

Oven mitts

Instructions

1. Preheat the oven to 450°F. If using a pizza stone, put it in the oven to preheat as well.
2. In a large bowl, dissolve the yeast and honey (or sugar) in the warm water. Let it stand for a few minutes, until the yeast becomes frothy.
3. Add the flour, olive oil, and salt, then stir with a wooden spoon or mix by hand until a fairly firm yet workable dough forms and is no longer sticky. If it is too sticky, mix in more flour, 1 tablespoon at a time. If it is too dry, mix in more water, 1 tablespoon at a time, until it reaches the desired texture.
4. For a thick crust, roll the dough into a ball; for a thin crust, roll the dough into two balls of equal size. For extra-thin crust or individual-sized pizzas, roll the dough into four balls of equal size.
5. Let the dough rest for 3 to 5 minutes while you gather your pizza toppings.

Instructions continued on next page.

6. Roll out the dough to your desired thickness and shape. Then, place the dough on a pizza stone dusted with cornmeal, a pizza pan, or a baking sheet lightly coated with olive oil. Pre-bake the crust until the top is light golden, about 5 minutes.
7. Remove the dough from the oven, top with your favorite pizza toppings, and bake until the crust is just browned and the toppings are bubbly, about 8 to 10 minutes. (Baking time will vary, depending on the thickness of the crust and the amount/type of toppings.)

Note: If you don't plan to use the dough right away, coat it with olive oil, put it in a zip-top bag, and store it in the refrigerator for up to 3 days or in the freezer for up to 1 month.

As you knead the dough, remember Carlo's love for Jesus and his dedication to using his talents to spread God's love.

Saint Cecilia

The Musical Martyr

Third century * Feast day: November 22

Patron of musicians, composers, instrument-makers, and poets

Whether it's an energetic song that gets you dancing or a soothing tune that calms you down, music has a special way of touching our hearts. For Cecilia, growing up in Rome, music was a way to praise God.

Even though Cecilia had taken a personal vow of chastity, her parents arranged for her to marry a young pagan nobleman named Valerian. During their wedding, as the music played, Cecilia sang her own hymn in her heart. It was a hymn of praise to God—a beautiful prayer to her true Spouse in heaven. Cecilia revealed to her new husband that she was a Christian and that she had made a vow of virginity to her heavenly Spouse. Valerian respected her devotion and soon converted to Christianity himself after seeing an angel by Cecilia's side! Soon after, Valerian's brother, Tiburtius, also converted.

In those times, it was very dangerous to be a Christian in Rome. Cecilia was arrested and asked to deny her faith, but she refused. She bravely faced many trials, and despite the dangers, she continued to sing praises to God. Legend has it that even in the final moments before her death, she sang to God with a joyful heart. Her courage and devotion inspired many others to embrace Christianity.

To celebrate St. Cecilia, enjoy these Crispy Baked Chicken Drumsticks. Just as Cecilia used her musical gifts to honor God, these drumsticks remind us of the joyful noise we can make in our own lives.

Saint Cecilia

Crispy Baked Chicken Drumsticks

Ingredients (SERVES 6)

6 medium chicken legs (drumsticks)
¼ cup unsalted butter, melted, or olive oil or avocado oil
½ teaspoon smoked paprika
½ teaspoon garlic powder
½ teaspoon sea salt
¼ teaspoon black pepper

Tools Checklist

Oven-safe rack
Baking sheet
Paper towels
Measuring cups
Measuring spoons
Pastry brush
Oven mitts

Instructions

1. Preheat the oven to 425°F. Place an oven-safe rack on top of a baking sheet.
2. Pat the chicken drumsticks dry with paper towels, which will help them get crispy, then arrange them on the rack.
3. Brush the chicken drumsticks with the melted butter, then season them with the smoked paprika, garlic powder, salt, and pepper.
4. Bake the drumsticks in the oven for 25 minutes. Flip them and bake for another 10 to 20 minutes, or until the internal temperature reaches 170°F.
5. Let the chicken rest for 5 minutes before serving.

Saint Andrew Kim Taegon

Korea's Courageous Priest

1821–1846 * Feast day: September 20

Patron of Korea

Has there ever been a time when you had to be very brave? Saint Andrew Kim Taegon, the first Korean-born Catholic priest, showed incredible courage in his life. Born in 1821 in Korea to a Christian family, Andrew felt a strong call to serve God. Even though it was extremely dangerous to be a Christian in Korea, his family's faith remained unshaken.

Andrew traveled more than a thousand miles to study in a seminary in China. He became a priest and returned to Korea to secretly bring the Christian faith to his people. His ministry in Korea was short-lived but abundantly fruitful. He offered the sacraments in secret, taught the faith, and coordinated the arrival of other missionary priests.

Andrew's activities did not go unnoticed. In 1846, he was arrested and punished to try to make him give up his faith. Despite the harsh treatment, Andrew remained strong and wrote several inspirational letters to his parishioners. He encouraged them to remain firm in their faith and find strength in the teachings of the Catholic Church.

Saint Andrew Kim Taegon's bravery and unwavering faith inspired many. He was martyred at the young age of twenty-five, but his legacy lives on. His letters and his example offered hope to his followers, reminding them that true faith cannot be stopped. The Korean rulers tried to stop the spread of Christianity, but they failed.

Saint Andrew Kim Taegon's life teaches us about courage, faith, and the power of standing up for what we believe in, even in the face of danger. To celebrate St. Andrew Kim Taegon, enjoy this Korean Beef Bowl. This flavorful dish is a nod to his Korean heritage and reminds us of his bravery and dedication.

Saint Andrew Kim Taegon, pray for us!

Korean Beef Bowl

Ingredients

(SERVES 6)

¼ cup low-sodium soy sauce or coconut aminos
2 tablespoons water
2 teaspoons light brown sugar
1 teaspoon sesame oil
½ teaspoon crushed red pepper flakes
1 pound lean ground beef
¼ cup chopped yellow onion
2 garlic cloves, crushed
1 teaspoon freshly grated ginger
3 cups cooked brown rice
1 small cucumber, skin on, sliced
½ tablespoon sesame seeds
2 sliced scallions, white and green parts

Tools Checklist

Measuring cups
Measuring spoons
Small bowl
Mixing spoons
Knives
Large, deep nonstick skillet with lid
Wooden spoon

Instructions

1. Combine the soy sauce (or aminos), 2 tablespoons water, brown sugar, sesame oil, and red pepper flakes in a small bowl.
2. Heat a large, deep nonstick skillet over high heat and add the ground beef. Cook, breaking the meat up with a wooden spoon, until cooked through, about 5 minutes.
3. Add the onion, garlic, and ginger and cook for 1 minute.
4. Pour the sauce over the beef, cover, and simmer on low heat for 10 minutes.
5. To assemble the bowls, place ¾ cup rice in each bowl, then top with 2/3 cup beef, several cucumber slices, and a sprinkling of sesame seeds and scallions.

Saint Florian

Faith and Fire

Around 250–304 * Feast day: May 4

Patron of chimney sweeps, soap-makers, and firefighters

Imagine a hero who fought fires and stood up for his faith. That's St. Florian, the patron saint of firefighters! Florian lived a long time ago, in the third century, in what is now Austria. He was an officer in the Roman army and had the important job of overseeing a group of soldiers whose task was to keep the city safe from fires.

Florian was not just brave in fighting fires; he was also brave in his faith. He was a Christian during a time when it was very dangerous to follow Jesus. The Roman Emperor Diocletian had ordered his soldiers to arrest and punish Christians.

When Florian heard that some of his fellow Christians had been captured, he knew he had to help them. He courageously declared his own faith and tried to protect them. This act of bravery led to his arrest.

The Roman officials tried to make Florian give up his faith, but he refused. Even though they threatened him, he stood firm and remained faithful to Jesus. Finally, Florian was sentenced to death, but his spirit of courage and protection lives on.

Saint Florian's story is a powerful example of bravery and faith. He showed that protecting others and standing up for what is right are actions that can make a big difference.

Today, firefighters all over the world look up to St. Florian as their protector and guide. This Firehouse Chili is the kind of meal firefighters love to share together. Chili is easy to make in big batches, hearty and filling after a long day, and perfect for gathering everyone around the table. As you cook and enjoy this warm, comforting dish, remember St. Florian's courage and say a prayer for all the brave people who work to keep us safe.

Saint Florian, pray for us!

Saint Florian

Firehouse Chili

Ingredients (SERVES 8 TO 10)

1½ pounds ground beef or ground turkey
1 large onion, chopped
1 clove fresh garlic, minced
1½ teaspoons salt, plus more to taste
¼ teaspoon cayenne pepper
¼ teaspoon ground cumin
¼ teaspoon ground oregano
2 tablespoons chili powder
2 (8-ounce) cans diced tomatoes with green chilies, undrained, hot or mild
1 (8-ounce) can tomato sauce
1 cup beef broth
2 (16-ounce) cans dark red kidney beans or chili-seasoned pinto beans, drained and rinsed

Tools Checklist

Large pot
Knives
Measuring spoons
Mixing spoons

Instructions

1. In a large pot, cook the ground beef until it is no longer pink. Drain the fat.
2. Add the remaining ingredients to the pot. Bring to a boil, then reduce the heat to simmer and cook for 30 to 45 minutes.
3. Serve hot with **Golden Cornbread** (see page 61) if desired.

Note: To make the chili in the crockpot, brown the meat and then add everything to the crockpot. Cook on low for 6 to 8 hours or on high for 3 or 4 hours.

Saint Joan of Arc

The Maid of Orléans

1412–1431 * Feast day: May 30

Patron of France, prisoners, people ridiculed for their piety, and soldiers

Did you know that a young girl once led the French army? That's the incredible story of St. Joan of Arc! Joan was born in a small village in France in 1412. From a young age, she felt a special connection to God, and she loved to pray. She began to hear voices and see visions of saints, who told her that she had a special mission.

When Joan was a teenager, these voices told her that she needed to help the king of France win the war against England. Imagine being so young and receiving such an important message! Joan was brave and full of faith. She went to see the king and convinced him to let her lead his army.

Dressed in armor and carrying a banner, Joan led the French troops into battle. She inspired the soldiers with her courage and faith. Her leadership helped the French win several important battles, and she became a hero in her country.

But Joan's story doesn't end there. Despite her successes, she was captured by the enemy and put on trial. The judges tried to make her deny that she heard the voices of saints, but Joan remained faithful and told the truth. She was sentenced to death. Joan died bravely, and her last words were a prayer to Jesus.

Years later, Joan was declared a saint because of her incredible faith, bravery, and dedication to God. Her story shows us that with faith and courage, we can overcome even the greatest challenges.

To celebrate St. Joan of Arc, try this French Lemon Chicken. Just as Joan's courageous spirit and fiery determination brought victory to France, this dish brings a burst of zest and warmth to your meal. Let her story inspire you to face your own challenges with the same fearless heart.

Saint Joan of Arc, pray for us!

French Lemon Chicken

Ingredients

(SERVES 6 TO 8)

1 lemon
2 tablespoons olive oil
2 tablespoons butter, softened
3 to 4 cloves garlic, minced
Salt and black pepper, to taste
1 whole chicken, approximately 3 pounds
½ medium yellow onion

Tools Checklist

Zester or small grater
Knives
Measuring spoons
Small bowl
Mixing spoons
Kitchen string or toothpicks
Shallow baking dish
Oven mitts

Instructions

1. Zest the yellow rind of the lemon. Cut the lemon in half and juice half of the lemon into a small bowl. Add the lemon zest, olive oil, butter, garlic, salt, and pepper. Stir well; the mixture should be fairly thick.
2. Gently lift the skin from the chicken breast and place about 1 tablespoon of the butter mixture under the skin. Massage it evenly across the breast.
3. Coat the skin of the chicken with the remaining butter mixture. Refrigerate for 30 to 45 minutes.
4. Preheat the oven to 425°F.
5. Slice the remaining lemon half and place it inside the chicken along with half of the onion. Tie the legs together with kitchen string or secure with toothpicks. Place the chicken in a shallow baking dish, breast side up, and place in the oven.
6. Turn the oven down to 375°F and bake for 1 hour and 15 minutes or until the inner thigh reaches an internal temperature of 165°F.
7. Let the chicken rest for at least 10 minutes before carving. Pour the pan juices over the meat and serve warm.

Saint André Bessette

The Humble Doorkeeper

1845–1937 * Feast day: January 6

Patron of the sick, the marginalized, those in need of healing, and family caregivers

Imagine being a humble doorkeeper who ends up changing the lives of thousands. That's the incredible story of St. André Bessette!

Born in Quebec, Canada, in 1845, André was the eighth of twelve children. Sadly, his parents died when he was young, leaving him an orphan at the age of twelve. Despite his hardships, André had deep faith in God and a heart full of kindness.

André was sickly as he grew up, which made it hard for him to keep a job because his health often got in the way. In 1870, at the age of twenty-five, he joined the Congregation of Holy Cross and was given the simple job of doorkeeper at Notre Dame College in Montreal. It was perfect for André.

As the doorkeeper, Brother André greeted visitors, cleaned the building, and ran errands, but what made him truly special was his devotion to St. Joseph. He often prayed with people, asking St. Joseph to intercede for them. Many people were healed through Brother André's prayers, and word of his healing powers spread quickly.

Soon, people from all over Canada came to see Brother André, seeking his prayers and blessings. Despite his growing fame, he remained humble and always gave credit to St. Joseph for the miracles. He saved his money and used donations to build a small chapel on Montreal's Mount Royal dedicated to St. Joseph, which eventually became Saint Joseph's Oratory, a famous shrine. More than a thousand crutches, canes, and braces have been left there by those who were healed.

This Doorkeeper's Meat Pie honors Brother André's role of welcoming all who came to his door. Meat pies are a traditional, comforting dish in Canada—warm, filling, and made for sharing. Brother André's life teaches us about the power of faith, humility, and kindness. He showed us that even the simplest acts of service can have a big impact when done with love and devotion.

Saint André Bessette, pray for us!

Doorkeeper's Meat Pie

Ingredients

(SERVES 8)

1 large potato, baked
1½ pounds ground pork
1 large onion, minced
½ cup water
½ teaspoon salt
½ teaspoon ground black pepper
½ teaspoon ground cinnamon
¼ teaspoon ground cloves
Pinch ground allspice
2 (9-inch) refrigerated pie crusts
1 large egg
¼ teaspoon paprika, or to taste

Tools Checklist

Potato masher
Measuring cups
Measuring spoons
Large skillet
Mixing spoons
Deep-dish pie plate
Pastry brush
Knife
Aluminum foil

Instructions

1. Mash the baked potato and place it into a large skillet with the ground pork, onion, water, salt, pepper, cinnamon, cloves, and allspice. Bring to a boil, then reduce the heat and simmer until very thick, at least 1 hour.
2. Preheat the oven to 350°F.
3. Line a deep-dish pie plate with one pie crust. Spoon in the pork and potato filling, then cover with remaining pie crust. Beat the egg and brush it over the pie crust, then sprinkle with paprika. Cut 4 slits, about ½ inch each, in the top crust to allow steam to escape.
4. Bake until the crust is well browned, about 50 minutes. If the edges brown too fast, cover them with a strip of foil.
5. Let the pie cool to almost room temperature before serving.

Saint José Luis Sánchez del Río

"Viva Cristo Rey!"

1913–1928 * Feast day: February 10
Patron of persecuted Christians and children

José Luis Sánchez del Río was a young hero who stood up for his faith. Born in 1913 in Mexico, José grew up during a time when the government was against the Catholic Church. Despite these challenges, José had a deep love for Jesus and a strong desire to defend his faith.

At just fourteen years old, José joined the *Cristeros*, a group fighting for religious freedom in Mexico. His parents worried about his safety, but José was determined to help. He became a flag-bearer for the Cristeros, showing his bravery and dedication.

One day, during a fierce battle, José was captured by government soldiers. They tried to force him to give up his faith, but José refused. Imprisoned and tortured, his faith remained unshaken. Even in the face of danger, José stood firm. He told his captors, "I will never give in. *Viva Cristo Rey*!" ("Long live Christ the King!")

The night before his martyrdom, José wrote a letter to his mother, expressing his love for her and his readiness to meet Jesus. The next day, he was led to his execution. As he walked, he continued to shout, "Viva Cristo Rey!" His bravery and faith inspired everyone who witnessed his final moments.

Although José Luis Sánchez del Río was only fourteen years old when he died, his courage and love for Jesus made him a hero and a saint. His story teaches us that no matter how young we are, we can stand up for what we believe in and make a difference.

This Slow-Cooker Pork Carnitas recipe honors St. José Luis' Mexican heritage, celebrating the rich, flavorful food shared by families and friends. As you prepare and enjoy this meal, remember his bravery, his deep love for his family and faith, and the strength it takes to stand up for what is right.

Saint José Luis Sánchez del Río, pray for us!

Slow-Cooker Pork Carnitas Tacos

Ingredients

(SERVES 6)

1 tablespoon chili powder
2 teaspoons ground cumin
2 teaspoons dried oregano
2 teaspoons salt
1 teaspoon ground black pepper
4 pounds pork shoulder, with excess fat trimmed
4 cloves garlic, peeled
2 onions, quartered
½ cup freshly squeezed orange juice
¼ cup freshly squeezed lime juice
Hard or soft taco shells
Taco fillings of your choice

Tools Checklist

Measuring cups
Measuring spoons
Small bowl
Knives
6-quart slow cooker
Forks
Large baking pan
Oven mitts

Instructions

1. In a small bowl, combine the chili powder, cumin, oregano, salt, and pepper. Season the pork shoulder with the spice mixture, rubbing it in thoroughly on all sides.
2. Place the garlic, onions, orange juice, lime juice, and seasoned pork shoulder into a 6-quart slow cooker. Cover and cook on low heat for 8 hours or high heat for 4 to 5 hours.
3. Remove the pork shoulder from the slow cooker and shred the meat before returning it to the pot with the juices; season with salt and pepper to taste, if needed. Cover and keep warm for another 30 minutes.
4. Preheat the oven to broil.
5. Place the shredded meat on a baking pan and broil until crisp and crusted, about 3 to 4 minutes.
6. Serve immediately in tacos with your favorite toppings, such as diced avocado, guacamole, pico de gallo, salsa, grated cheese, and sour cream.

Saint Paul Miki and Companions

Holy Heroes of Japan

Around 1562–1597 * Feast day: February 6

Patrons of Japan

Paul Miki was a brave man who stood up for his faith in Japan during a very dangerous time. Born in 1562 to a noble Japanese family, Paul Miki became a Jesuit. He was known for his powerful preaching and deep love for Jesus.

In the late 1500s, Japan's rulers began to fear the growing influence of Christianity. They started persecuting Christians, hoping to stop the spread of the faith. Despite the danger, Paul Miki continued to share the message of Jesus with everyone he met. His courage and dedication inspired many people to become Christians.

In 1597, Paul Miki and twenty-five other Christians, including priests, brothers, and laypeople, were arrested for their faith in Kyoto. They were then forced to walk 600 miles to the town of Nagasaki, where they would be executed. Along the way, they sang hymns, prayed, and encouraged each other to stay strong. When they reached Nagasaki, they were crucified on a hill, bravely facing their martyrdom.

Even as he hung on the cross, Paul Miki continued to preach. He forgave his persecutors and urged everyone to follow Jesus. His final words were filled with faith and hope, leaving a lasting impact on those who heard them. The unwavering faith and courage of St. Paul Miki and the other martyrs inspired many others to embrace Christianity, even in the face of persecution. Today, they are remembered as heroes who showed the world the power of faith and the strength of the human spirit.

To honor St. Paul Miki and his twenty-five companions, enjoy these delicious Yakitori Chicken Skewers. Just as this dish is a beloved part of Japanese cuisine, these martyrs are beloved figures in the history of the Church in Japan.

Saint Paul Miki and companions, pray for us!

Yakitori Chicken Skewers

Ingredients

(SERVES 6 TO 8)

For the sauce:

¼ cup soy sauce
½ cup plus 2 tablespoons water
¼ cup brown sugar
2 teaspoons minced garlic
2 teaspoons minced ginger
1 tablespoon honey
1 teaspoon toasted sesame oil
1 tablespoon rice vinegar
1 tablespoon plus 1 teaspoon cornstarch

For the chicken:

1¼ pounds chicken thighs or breasts, cut into bite-sized pieces
Salt and pepper, to taste
1 tablespoon vegetable oil
1 teaspoon sesame seeds
1 tablespoon sliced green onions

Tools Checklist

Measuring cups
Measuring spoons
Small pot
Mixing spoons
Small bowl
Knives
Wooden food skewers
Pastry brush
Outdoor grill or grill pan

Instructions continued on next page.

Instructions

For the sauce:

1. Place the soy sauce, ½ cup of water, brown sugar, garlic, ginger, honey, sesame oil, and rice vinegar in a small pot over medium-high heat. Stir until the sugar is dissolved, about 3 minutes. Then, turn up the heat to high and bring to a boil.
2. In a small bowl, mix the cornstarch with 2 tablespoons of cold water until dissolved. Add the cornstarch mixture to the sauce and boil for 1 to 2 minutes, or until the sauce has thickened.

For the chicken:

1. Soak 6 to 8 wooden skewers in cold water for at least 30 minutes before grilling.
2. Thread the uncooked chicken pieces onto the skewers. Season the chicken with salt and pepper to taste, then brush the vegetable oil over the chicken.
3. Preheat an outdoor grill or grill pan to medium heat.
4. Cook the chicken for 4 minutes per side, then brush the sauce over the chicken and cook for another 2 minutes per side.
5. Brush more sauce over the chicken, then cook for another minute per side.
6. Brush a final layer of sauce over the chicken, sprinkle with sesame seeds and green onions, and serve.

Note: While yakitori is often made on a grill, you can also cook the skewers in the oven if you prefer. To do so, follow steps 1 and 2, then place the chicken skewers on a sheet pan lined with foil coated with nonstick cooking spray. Broil for 4 minutes per side, then brush with more sauce and broil for another 4 minutes. Brush the chicken with another layer of sauce, then broil for 2 more minutes, and then finish the skewers as in step 6.

The unwavering faith and courage of St. Paul Miki and the other martyrs inspired many others to embrace Christianity, even in the face of persecution.

Saint Katharine Drexel

Champion of Education and Justice

1858–1955 * Feast day: March 3

Patron of racial justice and philanthropists

Katharine Drexel was an amazing woman who used her wealth to make a big difference in the world. Born in 1858 in Philadelphia, she could have lived a life of luxury and fun. Instead, Katharine decided to spend her fortune helping others, especially those who needed it most.

From a young age, Katharine was taught by her parents to care for others and to use her blessings to make the world a better place. As she grew up, she was deeply moved by the struggles of Native Americans and African Americans, who faced discrimination and a lack of education, and she saw her opportunity to help.

In 1889, after meeting with Pope Leo XIII, who encouraged her to become a missionary, Katharine founded the Sisters of the Blessed Sacrament. Katharine and her sisters traveled across the United States, building schools, churches, and hospitals to provide education and care for communities in need.

Throughout her life, no matter the challenges she faced, Katharine stayed strong in her faith and determination. She spent her entire fortune, around $20 million, to support her missions, and she inspired many others to join her cause. By the time of her death in 1955, she had established more than 60 schools and missions across the country.

Saint Katharine Drexel shows us how to be grateful for our blessings and use our time, talent, and treasure to glorify God. Her life teaches us the power of faith, generosity, and standing up for justice. She reminds us that we can all make a difference by serving others with love and compassion.

To celebrate St. Katharine Drexel, enjoy this delicious Sheet Pan Philly Cheesesteak. Katharine used her resources to nourish the minds and spirits of those she helped in her community and beyond, and this hearty dish brings together some of the favorite flavors of her city, Philadelphia.

Saint Katharine Drexel, pray for us!

Sheet Pan Philly Cheesesteak

Ingredients

(SERVES 4 TO 6)

2 tablespoons Worcestershire sauce
1½ tablespoons olive oil
1 teaspoon Dijon mustard
½ teaspoon garlic powder
½ teaspoon freshly ground black pepper
1 pound boneless ribeye steak
1 red bell pepper, thinly sliced
1 medium yellow onion, thinly sliced
1 long baguette
6 slices provolone cheese

Tools Checklist

Rimmed baking pan
Measuring spoons
Large, shallow dish
Mixing spoons
Knives
Meat thermometer
Cutting board
Medium bowl
Oven mitts

Instructions

1. Place a rimmed baking pan on the middle oven rack and preheat the oven to 475°F.
2. In a large, shallow dish, stir together the Worcestershire sauce, olive oil, mustard, garlic powder, and black pepper. Place the steak in the dish and turn it to coat it with sauce.
3. Place the steak in the middle of the hot baking sheet. Arrange the bell pepper and onion in an even layer around the steak, top it with the remaining marinade, and gently stir to coat.
4. Bake until a thermometer inserted in the center of the steak registers 135°F for medium-rare and the vegetables are tender, about 15 to 16 minutes. Transfer the steak to a cutting board and let rest for 5 minutes. Transfer the bell pepper and onion to a bowl. Thinly slice the steak against the grain and stir into the pepper and onion mixture.
5. Increase the oven temperature to broil. Place the baguette on a baking sheet and cut lengthwise, taking care not to cut all the way through. Place the cheese slices along both sides of the cut bread, then spoon the steak mixture on top of the cheese. Top with more cheese slices.
6. Broil until cheese is melted and the bread is toasted on the edges, about 1 to 2 minutes. Cut the sandwich into the desired number of servings.

Saint Josephine Bakhita

From Slavery to Sainthood

1869–1947 * Feast day: February 8

Patron of victims of human trafficking

Imagine being taken far away from home and treated badly, yet still finding the strength to smile and be kind. That's the incredible story of St. Josephine Bakhita!

Bakhita was born in Sudan, Africa, in 1869. As a young girl, she was kidnapped by slave traders and sold into slavery. She went through a lot of hard times. Her owners treated her well, but one day, the owners' son got very angry and hit Bakhita. She was injured so badly that she couldn't walk for a whole month. Later, she was sold to other people who treated her with cruelty, which was very painful and scary. But Bakhita never lost hope.

Eventually, she went to work for an Italian family, who treated her with kindness. They took her to Italy, where she learned about the Christian faith. Bakhita was so touched by the love and kindness of the Catholic Church that she decided to become a Christian. She was baptized and confirmed in 1890, taking the name Josephine.

Feeling a special call from God, Josephine joined the Canossian Sisters, a group of nuns dedicated to serving others. As a nun, she was known for her gentle spirit, joyful smile, and deep faith. She loved helping people, just as she had been helped.

Saint Josephine Bakhita's story teaches us about hope, forgiveness, and love. Even though she went through very hard times, she found peace and happiness in her faith. Her life shows us that no matter how tough things get, we can always find strength in God's love.

To celebrate St. Josephine Bakhita, enjoy this delicious African Chicken Stew. Just like Josephine brought warmth and love to everyone she met, this hearty stew brings the rich and comforting flavors of Africa to your table.

Saint Josephine Bakhita, pray for us!

African Chicken Stew

Ingredients (SERVES 8)

3 to 3½ pounds chicken, cut into pieces
Salt and pepper, to taste
1 to 2 teaspoons Creole seasoning
¼ to ½ cup olive oil
1 medium onion, sliced
3 to 4 cloves garlic, minced
2 cups tomato sauce
1½ teaspoon dried thyme
1 tablespoon smoked paprika
¼ teaspoon curry powder
1 bay leaf
2 cups chicken broth
1 to 2 cups sliced carrots
2 green onions, chopped
(white and green parts)
3 tablespoons parsley
2 cups cooked rice

Tools Checklist

Knives
Measuring spoons
Measuring cups
Large pot
Mixing spoons
Spatula

Instructions

1. Season the chicken with salt, pepper, and Creole seasoning. Set aside.
2. Heat the oil in a large pot over medium heat until hot, then add the chicken and sauté, stirring frequently and scraping any browned bits off the bottom of the pot, until the chicken is browned.
3. Add onion and garlic to the pot and sauté until tender, about 4 to 5 minutes.
4. Pour the tomato sauce into the pot of chicken, then add the thyme, smoked paprika, curry powder, bay leaf, and chicken broth. Bring to a boil, then reduce the heat and simmer until the chicken is tender, about 20 to 30 minutes. Stir frequently to prevent the stew from sticking to the bottom of the pot.
5. Add the carrots, green onions, and parsley. Cook for 5 more minutes. Adjust the thickness of the stew with water or stock if needed.
6. Season with salt to taste.
7. Remove the bay leaf and serve each portion of stew over ¼ cup of warm rice.

Chef Notes

Sweet Treats
"The past is no longer yours;
the future is not yet in your power.
You have only the present wherein to do good."
Saint Alphonsus Liguori

Saint Charles Lwanga and Companions

Faithful Friends

1860–1886 * Feast day: June 3

Patrons of African Catholic Youth Action, converts, and victims of torture

Standing up for what's right, even when it's tough, is something St. Charles Lwanga and his friends understood well. Charles Lwanga was born in Uganda, Africa, in 1860. He was a bright and brave young man who worked in the court of King Mwanga II. The king was not kind to Christians and treated them badly. Charles, along with many other young men in the king's court, had become Christians. They had been taught about Jesus by missionaries and had been baptized, learning to love and follow Christ.

The king didn't like this at all. He wanted everyone to follow his rules and beliefs. When he found out that Charles and his friends were Christians, he was furious. The king demanded that they give up their faith, but Charles and his companions refused. They knew that Jesus was their true King, and they couldn't turn away from him.

Because of their strong faith and refusal to deny Christianity, Charles and his friends were arrested. Although they were treated with cruelty, they remained strong and faithful to Jesus. Charles encouraged his friends to stay true to Jesus, and he prayed with them. Even though they were scared, they felt comfort in knowing they were doing the right thing.

In 1886, Charles and his companions were martyred for their faith. They showed incredible bravery and loyalty to God, becoming heroes and role models for Christians in their country and everywhere. Their story reminds us that faith can give us the courage to stand up for what is right, no matter how difficult it may be.

To celebrate the bravery and faith of St. Charles Lwanga and his companions, enjoy these delicious Ugandan Queen Cakes. Just as Charles and his friends found the sweetness of Jesus' love, these African treats remind us of the sweetness and strength we find in standing up for what we believe in.

Saint Charles Lwanga and companions, pray for us!

Ugandan Queen Cakes

Ingredients

(MAKES 12)

12 tablespoons butter, at room temperature
¾ cup sugar
3 eggs
1 cup all-purpose flour
1½ teaspoons baking powder
¾ teaspoon vanilla extract
1 teaspoon orange or lemon zest
Confectioners' sugar, for dusting

Tools Checklist

Measuring cups
Measuring spoons
Large and small bowls
Mixing spoons
Zester or small grater
12-cup muffin pan
Cupcake liners

Instructions

1. Preheat the oven to 350°F.
2. Beat the butter and sugar in a bowl until light and fluffy, about 5 minutes. Add the eggs one at a time, beating well until incorporated.
3. Combine the flour and baking powder in a small bowl, mix to combine, then add to the wet ingredients. Stir with a spoon to combine. Add the vanilla extract and orange or lemon zest and mix until incorporated.
4. Line a 12-cup muffin pan with cupcake liners and fill each about ¾ of the way with batter.
5. Bake for 25 minutes or until golden brown. Cool before lightly dusting the tops with confectioners' sugar.

Saint Alphonsus Liguori

The Practical Preacher

1696–1787 * Feast day: August 1

Patron of confessors and moral theologians; invoked for final perseverance and by those with scrupulosity or arthritis

Saint Alphonsus Liguori was born in Naples, Italy, in 1696. Growing up, Alphonsus was incredibly talented, excelling in his studies and becoming a successful lawyer by the age of sixteen. Everyone thought he had a bright future ahead, filled with wealth and fame.

Despite all his success, Alphonsus realized that true happiness wasn't found in winning court cases or gaining the admiration of others. He began to feel a deep calling to serve God in a more meaningful way. After much prayer and reflection, he made a courageous decision—he gave up his career as a lawyer and chose to become a priest.

As a priest, Alphonsus dedicated his life to helping people grow closer to God. He had a special gift for making Catholic teachings easy for everyone to understand. Alphonsus wrote many books and hymns and created sacred art that taught people about God's love, the importance of prayer, and the special role of Mary in our lives. His writings were so powerful and clear that they continue to inspire people today. Alphonsus believed that everyone, no matter who they were, had a special role in God's plan.

Alphonsus founded the Congregation of the Most Holy Redeemer, known as the Redemptorists. He wanted to gather priests and brothers who would dedicate their lives to preaching God's mercy, especially to the poor and those who felt forgotten. The Redemptorists traveled all over, sharing God's love and care. They continue this important mission today, sharing hope and faith with people everywhere.

Neapolitan ice cream originated in St. Alphonsus' hometown, Naples. Just like the ice cream, which combines chocolate, vanilla, and strawberry, Alphonsus's life was a blend of love for God, devotion to Mary, and joy in teaching others. Each part of his life added something special to the world, just like the different flavors of this sundae combine to make something delicious. He used his life to spread the sweetness of God's love, and you can use your talents to do the same!

Saint Alphonsus Liguori, pray for us!

Neapolitan Ice Cream Sundae

Ingredients (MAKES 1 SUNDAE)

1 scoop chocolate ice cream
1 scoop vanilla ice cream
1 scoop strawberry ice cream
Chocolate syrup
Whipped cream
Fresh strawberries, sliced
Crushed nuts (optional)
Maraschino cherry (optional)

Tools Checklist

Ice cream scoop
Tall glasses or bowls
Knife

Instructions

1. Place the scoop of chocolate ice cream at the bottom of a tall glass or bowl.
2. Add the scoop of vanilla ice cream on top of the chocolate.
3. Add the scoop of strawberry ice cream on top of the vanilla.
4. Drizzle chocolate syrup over the ice cream.
5. Add a generous swirl of whipped cream on top and garnish with the fresh strawberry slices.
6. Sprinkle crushed nuts over the whipped cream and top with a maraschino cherry, if desired.
7. Serve immediately.

Saint Martin de Porres

The Kindhearted Healer

1579–1639 * Feast day: November 3

Patron of mixed-race people, those seeking racial harmony, barbers, innkeepers, public health workers, and animals

Do you love helping others and sharing kindness? Saint Martin de Porres did just that throughout his life. Martin de Porres was born in Lima, Peru, in 1579. His father was a Spanish nobleman, and his mother was a freed slave from Africa. Life wasn't easy for Martin, because people often looked down on him due to his mixed heritage. However, Martin remained kind and loving to everyone he met.

As a young boy, Martin was apprenticed to a barber-surgeon, and he learned how to cut hair and treat wounds. He was known for his gentle touch and caring nature. Martin's deep faith led him to the Dominican Order, where he became a lay brother. He wanted to dedicate his life to helping others, especially the poor and sick.

Martin's kindness extended to all creatures, great and small. One of the best-known stories about him involves mice. The friary where he lived had a mouse problem. Instead of killing them, Martin talked to the mice and asked them to leave the building. Amazingly, they did! He even promised to feed them if they stayed outside, showing his compassion for all living beings.

Saint Martin worked tirelessly, caring for the sick, providing food and medicine to the poor, and even founding an orphanage and a hospital. He was known for performing miracles, such as healing the sick instantly and multiplying food to feed many people. His love and humility touched the hearts of everyone he met.

To celebrate St. Martin de Porres' gentle spirit and love for all creatures, enjoy making these Chocolate Cherry Mice. These cute and sweet treats remind us of Martin's kindness to all, even the smallest of God's creatures. As you enjoy them, remember to share your love and kindness with everyone around you.

Saint Martin de Porres, pray for us!

Chocolate Cherry Mice

Ingredients (MAKES 24)

24 stem-on maraschino or fresh cherries

2 cups semisweet milk chocolate or dark chocolate chips

1 tablespoon coconut oil, plus more if needed for consistency

24 milk chocolate or dark chocolate candy kisses, unwrapped

48 almond slices

Tools Checklist

Paper towels

Microwave-safe bowl or double boiler

Mixing spoons

Waxed or parchment paper

Instructions

1. Drain maraschino cherries or rinse fresh cherries and gently blot with paper towels.
2. In the microwave or on the stovetop on very low heat, melt the chocolate chips together with the coconut oil. Stir until smooth.
3. One at a time, hold each dry cherry by the stem and dip it into the chocolate mixture.
4. Place the chocolate-dipped cherries with stems up onto waxed or parchment paper to dry.
5. Reheat the remaining chocolate mixture to melt it again, if needed.
6. Press the bottom of a dipped cherry into the melted chocolate and then onto a chocolate candy kiss.
7. Press two almond slices, one on each side, between the chocolate kiss and the dipped cherry to make the mouse ears.
8. Allow the mice to sit in the refrigerator for a few minutes to set the chocolate before serving.

Saints Crispin and Crispinian

The Shoemaking Brothers

Third century * Feast day: October 25
Patrons of cobblers, curriers, tanners, and leatherworkers

Crispin and Crispinian were brothers who showed us how powerful kindness and humility can be. Born in Rome in the third century, they were strong in their Christian faith and dedicated to helping others. To support themselves and their mission, the brothers worked as shoemakers, and they were skilled craftsmen.

By night, the brothers made shoes to give away to the poor for free. By day, they preached the gospel in the streets, sharing the message of Christianity with anyone who would listen. Their charity, piety, and disregard for material things impressed the locals, leading many to convert to Christianity. Their humble tasks and occupations didn't stop them from making a big difference.

Crispin and Crispinian's growing popularity drew the attention of the Roman authorities, who were arresting Christians. The brothers were brought before the emperor and threatened, but they refused to give up their faith. Their courage and steadfastness inspired many.

In the end, Crispin and Crispinian were martyred for their faith, but their legacy of kindness and generosity lived on. They became the patron saints of shoemakers, and their story continues to inspire people to use their talents to help others. Their humble beginnings and lives show us that even simple acts of kindness can have a big impact.

To celebrate the generous spirit of Sts. Crispin and Crispinian, enjoy this Peach Berry Cobbler, a fun nod to the two shoemakers.

Saints Crispin and Crispinian, pray for us!

Peach Berry Cobbler

Ingredients

(SERVES 8)

¾ cup butter, cubed
1½ cups all-purpose flour
1½ cups sugar
3 teaspoons baking powder
¼ teaspoon salt
1¼ cups milk
½ teaspoon vanilla extract
3 cups fresh peach slices (see note)
1 cup fresh blueberries (see note)
2 teaspoons lemon juice
½ cup brown sugar
Vanilla ice cream, for serving

Tools Checklist

Knives
9 x 13-inch baking dish
Measuring cups and Measuring spoons
Medium bowl
Mixing spoons
Oven mitts

Instructions

1. Preheat the oven to 350°F.
2. Place the cubed butter in a 9 x 13-inch baking dish, then put it in the oven for a few minutes until the butter is melted.
3. In a medium bowl, combine the flour, sugar, baking powder, and salt. Add the milk and vanilla extract, then stir until smooth.
4. Pour the batter evenly over the melted butter in the pan, but do not stir. The melted butter will rise up over the batter.
5. Toss the peach slices and blueberries with the lemon juice, then spread them evenly over the batter—again, do not stir.
6. Sprinkle the brown sugar evenly over the fruit and batter, then bake until the top is golden brown, about 40 to 50 minutes.
7. Allow the cobbler to cool for a few minutes before serving with a scoop of vanilla ice cream.

Note: You may use frozen or canned peaches in place of fresh peaches. If using frozen peaches, thaw them first; if using canned peaches, drain them well. You may also use frozen blueberries instead of fresh; do not thaw them before using.

Saint Laura Montoya

A Teacher in the Jungle

1874–1949 * Feast day: October 21

Patron of orphans and those who suffer from racial discrimination

Saint Laura Montoya was born in 1874 in Jericó, Colombia. Her childhood was filled with both joy and sorrow. She was raised in a deeply Catholic family, and faith was the cornerstone of her life. When her father passed away in one of Colombia's civil wars, her family struggled financially. But Laura found comfort in prayer and her growing love for Jesus.

Despite having limited education, Laura was very smart and loved learning. When Laura was sixteen, her mother encouraged her to become a teacher. Laura not only taught school subjects but also shared the values of Christianity with her students.

As Laura continued teaching, she felt a powerful pull to serve those in need, especially the Indigenous people of Colombia. These communities faced many challenges and were often forgotten. Laura wanted to help them, respecting their unique cultures while sharing her faith.

In 1914, Laura and four women established the Congregation of the Missionary Sisters of Mary Immaculate and St. Catherine of Siena. Their mission was to serve the Indigenous communities with love and respect. Laura, fluent in several Indigenous languages, became a bridge between the Church and these communities. Laura and her sisters traveled into the jungles and mountains to set up schools and clinics. They believed education was key to empowering these communities.

Laura also became a relentless advocate for the rights of the Indigenous people, challenging discriminatory practices and working for better living conditions. Her gentle yet strong voice earned her the respect of both the Indigenous communities and government officials.

To celebrate St. Laura Montoya's dedication and love, enjoy this delicious Colombian Natilla Custard. Just as St. Laura brought sweetness and hope to many lives, this traditional dessert brings a taste of Colombia's rich heritage to your table.

Saint Laura Montoya, pray for us!

Colombian Natilla Custard

Ingredients

(SERVES 8 TO 10)

3 cups whole milk
1 cup plus 2 tablespoons cornstarch
1 cup coconut milk
1/2 cup shredded coconut
2 cinnamon sticks
1 (14-ounce) can condensed milk
1/3 cup sugar
Pinch salt
1/2 teaspoon vanilla extract
1 tablespoon butter
Ground cinnamon, to taste

Tools Checklist

Measuring cups and Measuring spoons
Small bowl
Mixing spoons
Blender
Medium pot
Wooden spoon
Dessert molds

Instructions

1. Place 1 cup of milk in a small bowl, add the cornstarch, and stir to dissolve. Set aside.
2. Blend the coconut milk and shredded coconut in a blender until smooth. Set aside.
3. Place the remaining 2 cups of milk and the cinnamon sticks in a medium pot and bring the mixture to a boil over medium-low heat. When the milk is warm but not boiling, add the coconut mixture.
4. When the milk starts boiling, add the condensed milk, sugar, and salt. Mix well with a wooden spoon. Add the cornstarch mixture and continue stirring constantly.
5. Add the vanilla extract. Reduce the heat to low and continue stirring until the mixture thickens, about 10 to 20 minutes. Add the butter, mix, and remove from heat. Remove the cinnamon sticks.
6. Spoon the custard into a large mold or individual dessert molds.
7. Sprinkle ground cinnamon on top and let the custard cool to room temperature for at least 2 hours, then refrigerate until ready to serve.

Blessed Peter To Rot

A Capable Catechist

1912–1945 * Feast day: July 7

Patron of married couples and catechists

Peter To Rot was born in 1912 in Papua New Guinea. As a boy, he was like most other kids—serving at Mass, playing sports, helping with chores, and occasionally getting into mischief. What made him stand out was his natural leadership. Even though he was the chief's son, he was kind and never bossy. Peter was agile at climbing coconut trees, and he often helped the older villagers by gathering coconuts for them.

Inspired by his faith, Peter decided to become a catechist to teach others about Jesus. He was known for his kindness, gentleness, and dedication. Peter's commitment to his faith was unwavering, especially during World War II, when the Japanese occupied Papua New Guinea and banned Christian practices. Despite the danger, Peter continued to hold secret services, baptize babies, and help his community keep their faith alive.

Peter was also a devoted husband and loving father. He married in 1936 and valued the sanctity of marriage. He spoke out against the Japanese practice of taking multiple wives, standing up for religious values and the teachings of Christ. His faith was his guiding light, and daily Mass, holy Communion, and frequent prayers gave him the strength and wisdom to counsel others.

During the war, Peter was entrusted with the local parish. Even when he was arrested and pressured to stop his religious activities, he remained steadfast. He was a true example of living a Christian life with purity and joy, inspiring others to do the same. His courage and devotion eventually led to his martyrdom in 1945.

To honor Blessed Peter To Rot, enjoy these Chewy Coconut Cookies. Peter's habit of climbing coconut trees to help others reflects his spirit of service and love. As you enjoy these cookies, remember his courage and dedication to his Christian faith.

Blessed Peter To Rot, pray for us!

Chewy Coconut Cookies

Ingredients

(MAKES 36)

1¼ cups all-purpose flour
½ teaspoon baking soda
¼ teaspoon salt
½ cup butter
½ cup brown sugar, packed
½ cup white sugar
1 egg
½ teaspoon vanilla extract
1 1/3 cups flaked coconut

Tools Checklist

Measuring cups
Measuring spoons
Large and medium bowls
Mixing spoons
Electric mixer
Baking sheets
Oven mitts
Wire cooling rack

Instructions

1. Preheat the oven to 350°F.
2. Combine the flour, baking soda, and salt in a medium bowl and set aside.
3. With an electric mixer, beat the butter, brown sugar, and white sugar together in a large bowl until smooth. Add the egg and vanilla, then beat until light and fluffy.
4. Gradually blend in the flour mixture, then stir in the coconut until well combined.
5. Drop the dough by teaspoonfuls, about 3 inches apart, onto ungreased baking sheets.
6. Bake until golden brown, about 8 to 10 minutes.
7. Allow the cookies to cool briefly on the baking sheets before transferring them to a wire rack to cool completely before serving.

Saint Joseph of Cupertino

The Flying Friar

1603–1663 * Feast day: September 18

Patron of aviation, astronauts, those with intellectual disabilities, test-taking, and students

Have you ever felt like you didn't quite fit in? Maybe you've stumbled, dropped things, or daydreamed when you should have been focusing. If so, you're not alone! There is a saint named Joseph of Cupertino who felt just the same way.

Joseph was born in Naples in 1603. When he was young, people began to notice that sometimes he seemed to be in his own world. He was forgetful and sometimes a little uncomfortable in social situations. But Joseph had a heart full of love and a deep connection to God.

Joseph wanted to be a priest, but the road was not easy. He struggled with his studies, and even the monks had a hard time believing in him at first. But Joseph knew that God had a special plan for him, and he never gave up.

With hard work and faith, Joseph became a priest, and that's when wonderful things began to happen. While praying, he would become so lost in his love for God that his feet would lift off the ground! He would float in the air, filled with joy, feeling God's embrace.

People came from all over to witness this extraordinary connection Joseph had with God. They wanted to see the boy who could float during prayer and lift heavy objects as if they were feathers. But, more than that, they wanted to hear Joseph's wise words and feel the love he had for everyone he met.

When you taste a delicious piece of Sky-High Lemon Pie, think of St. Joseph of Cupertino. If you ever feel a bit left out or find something hard to do, remember his incredible journey. His story of persistence and dedication might lift your heart and inspire you to reach for the sky too!

Saint Joseph of Cupertino, pray for us!

SUGAR

Sky-High Lemon Meringue Pie

Ingredients

(SERVES 8)

For the filling:

1 cup sugar
2 tablespoons all-purpose flour
3 tablespoons cornstarch
¼ teaspoon salt
1½ cups water
2 lemons, juiced and zested
2 tablespoons butter
4 egg yolks, beaten
1 (9-inch) pie crust, baked, in pie pan

For the meringue:

4 egg whites, at room temperature
¼ teaspoon cream of tartar
½ cup sugar

Tools Checklist

Measuring cups
Measuring spoons
Medium saucepan
Whisk
Mixing spoons
Small bowl
Glass, metal, or ceramic bowl
Rubber spatula
Oven mitts

Instructions

For the filling:

1. Preheat the oven to 350°F.
2. Whisk the sugar, flour, cornstarch, and salt together in a medium saucepan, then stir in the water, lemon juice, and lemon zest. Cook over medium-high heat, stirring frequently, until the mixture comes to a boil. Add the butter and stir it into the mixture.
3. Place the egg yolks in a small bowl and gradually whisk in ½ cup of the hot sugar mixture. Then, whisk the egg-yolk mixture back into the rest of the sugar mixture.
4. Bring to a boil and continue to cook while stirring constantly until the mixture is thick.
5. Remove from the heat and pour the filling into the baked pie crust.

Instructions continued on next page.

For the meringue:

1. Beat the egg whites in a glass, metal, or ceramic bowl until glossy and smooth, then add the cream of tartar and beat until combined. Gradually add the sugar, continuing to beat until stiff peaks form.
2. Spread the meringue over the pie filling to the edges of the crust, covering the pie filling completely.
3. Bake in the preheated oven about 4 inches below the heat until golden, about 10 minutes.
4. Let the pie cool completely at room temperature, then chill it in the refrigerator for 2 hours (or longer) before serving.

If you ever feel a bit left out or find something hard to do, remember the incredible journey of Saint Joseph of Cupertino.

Saint Thomas More

The Courageous Counselor

1478–1535 * Feast day: June 22

Patron of politicians, government leaders, lawyers, and widowers

Saint Thomas More was a man of great faith and integrity who stood up for what he believed, even when it cost him everything. Born in London in 1478, Thomas was a brilliant student who loved to learn. He became a lawyer, a writer, and a trusted advisor to King Henry VIII. Thomas was very successful in his career, but he always put God and his faith first.

Thomas was known for his sense of humor and kindness. He loved spending time with his family and friends, sharing stories and laughter. But his life took a serious turn when King Henry VIII wanted to divorce his wife and remarry, which was against the Church's teachings. Thomas refused to support the king's decision and stood firm in his faith, even though it meant losing his position and wealth.

The king was furious and had Thomas imprisoned in the Tower of London. Even in prison, Thomas remained cheerful and prayed constantly. He wrote letters to his family, encouraging them to stay strong in their faith. Thomas' bravery and devotion to God inspired many people around him.

Eventually, Thomas was put on trial and sentenced to death. He faced his fate with courage, knowing that he had stayed true to his beliefs. On the day of his execution, he famously said, "I die the king's good servant, but God's first." Thomas More was martyred on July 6, 1535, for refusing to betray his faith.

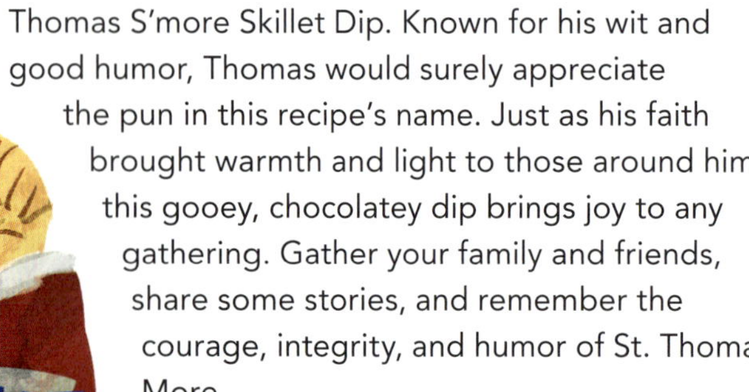

To celebrate St. Thomas More, enjoy this delicious Thomas S'more Skillet Dip. Known for his wit and good humor, Thomas would surely appreciate the pun in this recipe's name. Just as his faith brought warmth and light to those around him, this gooey, chocolatey dip brings joy to any gathering. Gather your family and friends, share some stories, and remember the courage, integrity, and humor of St. Thomas More.

Saint Thomas More, pray for us!

Thomas S'more Skillet Dip

Ingredients

(SERVES 8)

½ tablespoon butter
1¾ cups milk chocolate chips
½ cup mini marshmallows
Graham crackers, for serving

Tools Checklist

10-inch skillet
Pastry brush
Measuring cups
Measuring spoons
Oven mitts
Trivet

Instructions

1. Preheat the oven to 450°F and set a rack in the middle.
2. On your stovetop, heat a 10-inch skillet over low heat. When the skillet is warm, add the butter to the skillet to melt. Once the butter is melted, use a pastry brush to coat the sides and bottom of the skillet.
3. Turn off the heat, add the chocolate chips, and top with a thin layer of marshmallows.
4. Bake on the middle rack until the tops of the marshmallows are golden brown, about 5 to 6 minutes.
5. Carefully transfer the hot skillet to a trivet. Serve the dip warm with graham crackers.

Saint Philip Neri

Humor and Humility

1515–1595 * Feast day: May 26

Patron of humor and joy

Imagine a saint who could make you laugh while leading you closer to God! That was St. Philip Neri, known as the "Laughing Saint." Born in Florence, Italy, in 1515, Philip was a bright and energetic child who loved to spread joy wherever he went. From a young age, he was full of playful jokes and funny stories, making everyone around him smile. His joyful spirit and sense of humor were as much a part of his saintly nature as his deep love for God and desire to help others.

As a young man, Philip moved to Rome, where he dedicated his life to serving the poor and sick. He founded the Congregation of the Oratory, a community of priests who shared his passion for helping others and spreading joy. Philip's unique approach to faith included music, laughter, and games, making his gatherings full of happiness and inspiration for many.

Philip's joy was contagious. He believed that laughter and lightheartedness were essential parts of a healthy spiritual life. His playful antics often surprised those around him, but they also drew people closer to God. Philip once shaved off half of his beard before an important meeting to remind everyone not to take themselves too seriously.

Despite his humorous nature, Philip was very humble and deeply committed to his faith. He spent long hours in prayer and had a profound love for the Eucharist. People flocked to him for confession and guidance because they knew that he combined wisdom with a light heart.

Saint Philip Neri's life teaches us that faith doesn't have to be solemn and serious all the time. Joy and laughter are important in our spiritual lives. His example reminds us to find joy in our faith and to spread that joy to others.

To celebrate St. Philip Neri's joyful spirit, enjoy these Snickering Saint Snickerdoodles. Just as Philip brought laughter and love to those around him, these delightful cookies are sure to bring smiles to your family and friends.

Saint Philip Neri, pray for us!

Snickering Saint Snickerdoodles

Ingredients

(MAKES ABOUT 24)

For the cinnamon-sugar mixture:

¼ cup sugar
1½ tablespoons cinnamon

For the cookies:

1 cup unsalted butter, softened
1½ cups sugar
2 large eggs
2 teaspoons vanilla extract
2¾ cups all-purpose flour
1 teaspoon cream of tartar
½ teaspoon baking soda
1 teaspoon salt

Tools Checklist

Measuring cups
Measuring spoons
Large and small bowls
Mixing spoons
Rubber spatula
Plastic wrap
Baking sheets
Parchment paper
Oven mitts
Wire cooling racks

Instructions

For the cinnamon-sugar mixture:

1. In a small bowl, stir together the sugar and cinnamon. Set aside.

For the cookies:

1. Preheat the oven to 350°F.
2. In a large mixing bowl, cream the butter and sugar together for 4 to 5 minutes until light and fluffy. Scrape the sides of the bowl and add the eggs and vanilla. Cream for 1 to 2 minutes longer.
3. Stir in the flour, cream of tartar, baking soda, and salt until just combined.
4. Wrap the dough tightly with plastic wrap and let it refrigerate for 20 to 30 minutes.

Instructions continued on next page.

5. Remove the dough from the refrigerator and use a 2-tablespoon cookie scoop to make balls of dough.
6. Drop each dough ball into the cinnamon-sugar mixture and completely coat it.
7. Place the dough balls on a baking sheet lined with parchment paper. Gently press down in the center of each ball if you want flatter cookies.
8. Bake for 9 to 11 minutes, or until golden around the edge and barely set in the middle.
9. Let the cookies cool on the baking sheets for 5 minutes to set before transferring them to wire racks to cool completely.

Just as Philip brought laughter and love to those around him, these delightful cookies are sure to bring smiles to your family and friends.

Saint Anna Wang

The Brave Girl of China

1886–1900 * Feast day: July 22

Patron of young people, the innocent, and China

Imagine being so brave and so dedicated to your faith that you inspire everyone around you, even though you're just a kid. That's the amazing story of St. Anna Wang! Born in 1886 in the Xingtai Hebei Province in China, Anna was a young person with big dreams and a loving family. From a very young age, Anna's faith was incredibly strong. At only ten years old, she made the huge decision to dedicate her entire life to God.

As a teenager, Anna faced unimaginable challenges. In 1900, during the Boxer Rebellion, Christians in China were persecuted, and Anna's village was attacked. She was just fourteen years old when soldiers came to her home and demanded that she give up her faith. Anna was terrified, but she refused to deny Jesus. Her steadfast faith angered the soldiers, and they threatened her with death.

Anna was taken, along with other Christians, to a place of execution. Even at such a young age, she demonstrated remarkable bravery and led the others in prayer. When she was given a final chance to save her life by rejecting her faith, she boldly declared, "The door of heaven is open to all" and refused to betray Jesus. Her fearlessness moved many of the people, and her unwavering commitment to her faith in the face of death is a powerful example of courage and dedication.

Saint Anna Wang's story shows us that faith and bravery can shine brightly, even in the darkest of times. She reminds us that standing up for what we believe in, no matter how young we are, is a powerful act of love and devotion. We can all be saints and make a big difference.

To celebrate St. Anna Wang's incredible courage and faith, enjoy this refreshing Mandarin Orange Sherbet. Just as Anna's faith brought light and hope to those around her, this sweet and tangy treat made with a popular Chinese fruit can bring a burst of joy to your day.

Saint Anna Wang, pray for us!

Saint Anna Wang

Mandarin Orange Sherbet

Ingredients

(SERVES 6)

3 cups clementine segments, frozen
¼ cup canned coconut milk (preferred) or regular milk
2 tablespoons honey
1 tablespoon vanilla extract
Dark chocolate drizzle, for garnish (optional)

Tools Checklist

Measuring cup
Measuring spoons
Food processor
Rubber spatula
Ice cream scoop

Instructions

1. Add the frozen clementine segments, coconut milk (or milk of choice), honey, and vanilla extract to a food processor. Blend the ingredients together for a few minutes, scraping down the sides as needed, until the sherbet is smooth and creamy, similar to the texture of soft-serve ice cream.
2. Immediately scoop the sherbet into bowls, garnish with dark chocolate drizzle if desired, and serve.

Chef Notes

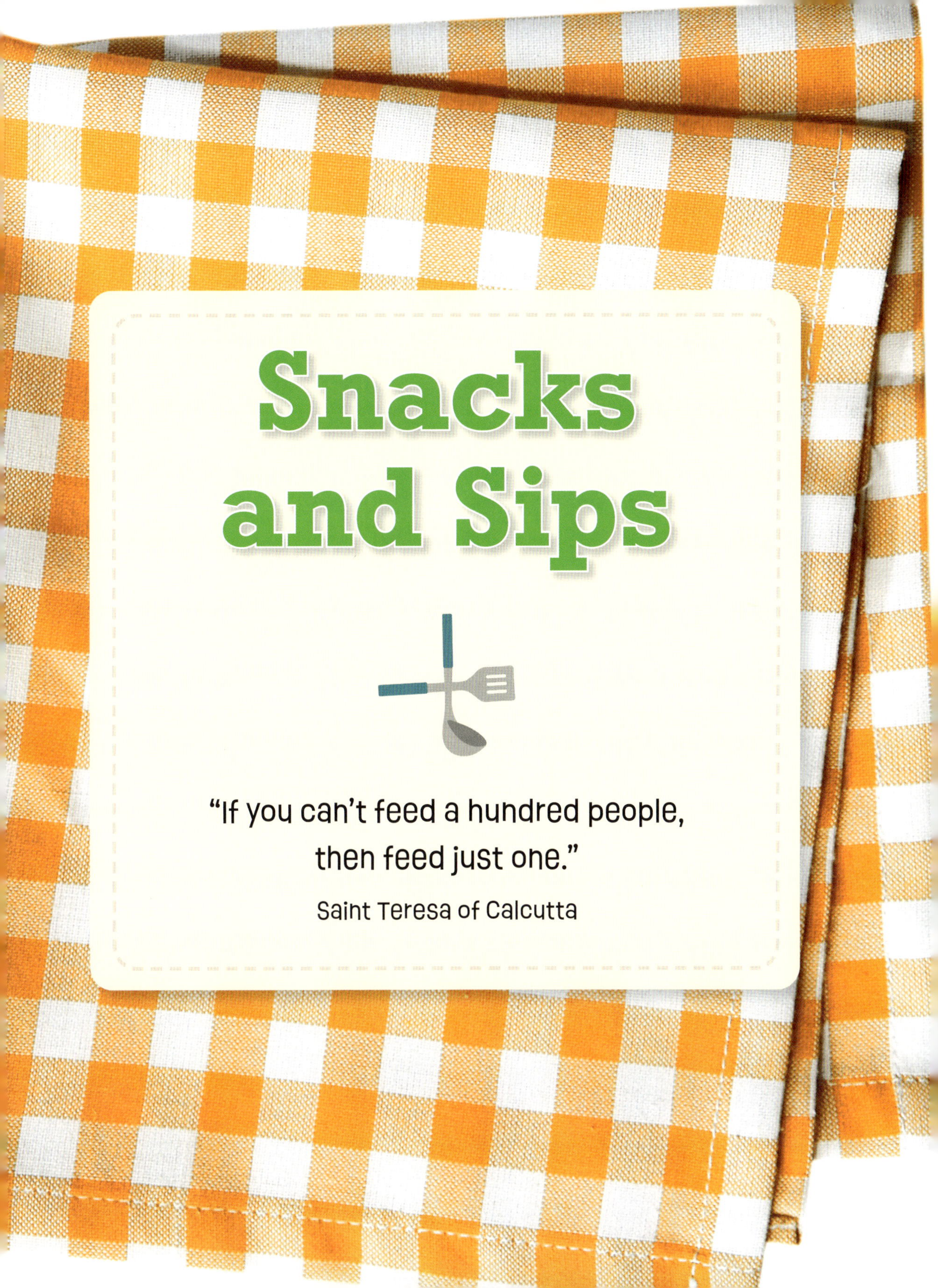

Snacks and Sips

"If you can't feed a hundred people, then feed just one."

Saint Teresa of Calcutta

Saints Timothy and Maura

The Newlywed Martyrs

Third century * Feast day: May 3
Patrons of married couples

The story of Sts. Timothy and Maura is one of incredible bravery and love. They were a young couple who lived in Egypt a long time ago, in the third century. Timothy was a lector in the church, and he helped spread the word of God. Maura, his wife, shared his strong faith. They had just gotten married, but their happiness was soon challenged by the Roman authorities, who didn't like Christians.

Only twenty days after their wedding, Timothy was arrested because he refused to give up the sacred Scriptures that he was protecting. The Romans tortured him, trying to make him change his mind, but Timothy's faith was too strong. When Maura was brought before the authorities, they hoped she would convince Timothy to give in. But instead, Maura encouraged him to stay strong, telling him that their faith was more important than anything else.

Seeing Maura's courage, the authorities decided that Timothy and Maura would be crucified together, but, no matter what, Timothy and Maura held onto their faith and each other. Their love for God and for one another gave them the strength to face anything, even death. Timothy and Maura were crucified facing each other. For ten days, they prayed together, sang hymns, and encouraged each other as they suffered for Christ. When one was weak, the other would be strong, reminding each other of what Christ suffered and the promise of life in heaven. Their story shows us that true love and faith can make us brave and keep us strong, even when things are very hard.

To celebrate Sts. Timothy and Maura, enjoy this Egyptian Yogurt Cucumber Dip. Just like their faith was strong and refreshing, this dip is a flavorful, cool treat that reminds us of the saints' homeland.

Saints Timothy and Maura, pray for us!

Saints Timothy and Maura

Egyptian Yogurt and Cucumber Dip

Ingredients

(SERVES 6 TO 8)

4 to 5 cups diced cucumber (skin on)
3 cups plain Greek yogurt
Juice of 1 to 1½ large lemons
1 clove garlic, minced
Sea salt, to taste
Coarse ground pepper, to taste
Extra-virgin olive oil, optional
Red chili flakes, optional

Tools Checklist

Knives
Paper towels
Measuring cups
Juicer (optional)
Large bowl
Mixing spoons

Instructions

1. Squeeze the excess liquid out of the cucumber with your hands and dab the moisture off with a paper towel.
2. Combine the cucumber, Greek yogurt, lemon juice, and minced garlic in a large mixing bowl.
3. Season with salt and a pinch of black pepper. Top with a little extra-virgin olive oil or red chili flakes, if desired.
4. Serve as a dip with chips, vegetables, or pita or as a topping on sandwiches.

Saint John the Baptist

Preparing the Way for God

Around 4 BC to around 30 AD * Feast day: June 24

Patron of builders, baptism, converts, lambs, monastics, printers, tailors, the sick, nurses, booksellers, heart patients, firefighters, and more

Even before he was born, John was chosen by God to prepare the way for Jesus. His mother, Elizabeth, was visited by the angel Gabriel, who told her she would have a son who would be filled with the Holy Spirit from birth. When John grew up, he lived a simple and humble life in the desert, wearing clothes made of camel's hair and eating locusts and wild honey.

John was fearless in his preaching, calling people to repent and turn back to God. He baptized many in the Jordan River, telling them to prepare their hearts for the coming of the Messiah. His message was powerful, and people from all over came to hear him speak. But John always made it clear that he was not the Messiah—he was just the messenger, preparing the way for Jesus.

One of the most remarkable things about John was his humility. Even though he had many followers, he knew his mission was to point others to Jesus. When Jesus came to be baptized, John recognized him immediately and said, "Behold, the Lamb of God!" John's whole life was dedicated to making sure people were ready to meet Jesus.

John's courage and dedication eventually led to his martyrdom. He was imprisoned and later beheaded because he spoke out against the wrongdoings of King Herod. But even in death, John's life was a testament to his unwavering faith and his role in God's plan.

To celebrate St. John the Baptist, enjoy these Peanut Butter Stuffed Dates. Just as John's simple diet of locusts and wild honey sustained him in the desert, these satisfying treats remind us of the strength we find in faith and simplicity.

Saint John the Baptist, pray for us!

Peanut Butter Stuffed Dates

Ingredients

(MAKES 12)

12 Medjool dates

1/3 cup all-natural smooth peanut butter

1/2 cup semisweet chocolate chips

1 teaspoon coconut oil

Pinch flaky sea salt (optional)

Tools Checklist

Baking sheet

Parchment paper

Knife

Small bowl

Mixing spoons

Instructions

1. Line a baking sheet with parchment paper. Cut a slit in the center of each date, lengthwise, being careful not to cut all the way through. Remove the pits.
2. Stuff the inside of each date generously with peanut butter and place it on the baking sheet.
3. In a small bowl, combine the chocolate chips and coconut oil. Melt in the microwave in 30-second increments, mixing it with a spoon after each 30 seconds, until smooth and combined. Drizzle the melted chocolate over the dates to coat, then sprinkle with sea salt (optional).
4. Refrigerate the stuffed dates until the chocolate has fully hardened, about 30 minutes, before serving.

Saint Teresa of the Andes

Flower of the Andes

1900–1920 * Feast day: July 13

Patron of Santiago, young people, and the sick

Juana Fernandez Solar was a joyful and spirited young girl who grew up in Santiago, Chile, in the early 1900s. As a child, she loved sports and spending time with her family, but her heart was always drawn to God. One day, she read the autobiography of the French-born St. Thérèse of Lisieux, known as the "Little Flower." This book inspired Juana, deepening her desire to serve God and helping her understand the path she was meant to follow.

At the age of nineteen, Juana entered the Carmelite convent, taking the name Teresa. The convent offered the simple lifestyle Teresa longed for and the joy of living in a community of women completely devoted to God. She spent her days in prayer and sacrifice, finding peace and purpose in her new life. "I am God's," she wrote in her diary. "He created me and is my beginning and my end."

Teresa's time in the convent was short, because she was diagnosed with a serious illness not long after joining, but her faith remained strong. She embraced her suffering with joy, offering it to God and inspiring those around her with her unwavering devotion. Teresa began a mission of letter-writing, sharing her thoughts on the spiritual life with many people. She passed away just a year later, in 1920, but her life left a lasting impact on those who knew her. She became the first Chilean to be canonized, and her story continues to inspire young people to live lives of faith and joy.

To honor St. Teresa of the Andes, enjoy this refreshing Chilean Strawberry Punch. Just as Teresa's life was filled with sweetness and devotion, this delicious drink reminds us to cherish the simple joys that bring us closer to God.

Saint Teresa of the Andes, pray for us!

Chilean Strawberry Punch

Ingredients

(SERVES ABOUT 6)

1½ to 2 cups strawberries, stems removed, chopped, plus whole strawberries for garnish (optional)

½ cup fresh lime juice (4 to 5 limes) tablespoon lime juice

½ cup fresh mint leaves, plus more for garnish (optional)

3 to 4 tablespoons honey or maple syrup (depending on desired sweetness)

Ice cubes or crushed ice, enough to fill the pitcher about halfway

2 liters sparkling water (strawberry flavored or regular)

Lime slices, for garnish (optional)

Tools Checklist

Knives

Measuring cups

Measuring spoons

Large pitcher

Wooden spoon

Instructions

1. In a large pitcher, combine the chopped strawberries, lime juice, mint leaves, and honey (or syrup). Use a wooden spoon to gently muddle (see note) the fruit and mint.
2. Fill the pitcher about halfway with ice, then fill it the rest of the way with sparkling water. Stir gently to combine all ingredients.
3. Garnish with whole strawberries, extra mint leaves, and lime slices, if desired.
4. Serve in glasses over more ice, if desired.

Note: To muddle ingredients in a drink means to mash them so that they release their juices and flavors.

Saint Matthew

A Change of Heart

First century * Feast day: September 21

Patron of accountants, bankers, bookkeepers, security guards, and stockbrokers

Matthew was a tax collector before he met Jesus, which meant he wasn't very popular. People often saw tax collectors as greedy and untrustworthy because they worked for the Roman government, taking money from their fellow Jews. But Matthew's life changed forever when Jesus saw him sitting at his tax booth and said, "Follow me." Without hesitation, Matthew got up, left everything behind, and followed Jesus.

Matthew became one of Jesus' Twelve Apostles, traveling with him, learning from him, and witnessing his miracles. Despite his past, Matthew was chosen to spread the Good News. He even wrote one of the four gospels, sharing the story of Jesus' life, death, and resurrection with the world. Matthew's Gospel is full of teachings that remind us to love God and our neighbors, showing that no matter where we start, we can always turn our lives around with God's help.

Saint Matthew's story teaches us that everyone has a place in God's plan, no matter their past. He reminds us that Jesus sees the good in everyone and can transform even the most unlikely people into his closest followers.

To celebrate St. Matthew, enjoy these Sweet Potato Coins. Just as Matthew traded his old life of collecting coins for a life of following Jesus, these Sweet Potato Coins remind us that true value isn't in what we have, but in how we live and who we follow.

Saint Matthew, pray for us!

Saint Matthew

Sweet Potato Coins

Ingredients (SERVES 8)

1/3 cup olive oil
1 tablespoon dried rosemary
1 teaspoon salt
1 teaspoon black pepper
1 1/2 pounds sweet potatoes

Tools Checklist

Two baking sheets
Parchment paper
Measuring cups
Measuring spoons
Large bowl
Mixing spoons
Mandoline or knife
Oven mitts
Wire cooling racks

Instructions

1. Preheat the oven to 400°F. Line 2 large baking sheets with parchment paper and set aside.
2. Combine the olive oil, rosemary, salt, and pepper in a large mixing bowl.
3. Peel the sweet potatoes, then use a mandoline slicer or knife to cut them into thin rounds.
4. Add the sliced sweet potatoes to the bowl and toss to coat them with the olive oil mixture.
5. Spread the sweet potato slices on the baking sheets in a single layer, leaving space around each one. Bake for 10 to 12 minutes, turn them over, and bake for another 10 to 12 minutes, until golden.
6. Remove from the oven and cool the sweet potato rounds on wire racks for about 5 to 10 minutes before serving. (They will become more crisp as they cool.)

Saint Teresa of Calcutta

A Sip of Kindness

1910–1997 * Feast day: September 5

Patron of World Youth Day and the Missionaries of Charity

Born Agnes Gonxha Bojaxhiu in what is now North Macedonia, the saint commonly known as Mother Teresa was a woman of compassion, dedicated to serving the poor and the forgotten. Her heart was filled with an overwhelming desire to quench the spiritual thirst of those in need. Her mission took her to the bustling streets and slums of Kolkata (formerly Calcutta), India, where her love knew no bounds.

"I thirst"—to Mother Teresa, this powerful phrase was more than just an expression; it was a call to action. She saw Jesus in the face of every person she helped, and she believed in easing their physical thirst as well as their spiritual longing.

Imagine the hot and dusty streets of Kolkata. The sun beats down as Mother Teresa and her fellow sisters walk from home to home to care for the sick and the hungry. The sisters and the people they helped needed something to refresh and rejuvenate their tired bodies.

Mother Teresa's hands, though small, were mighty in their ability to heal and comfort. She understood the importance of small acts of kindness, whether it was a smile, a touch, or a refreshing drink to a weary soul. Her story teaches us that love and compassion are the essential ingredients in every aspect of our lives.

Made with ginger to soothe the stomach, a splash of tart apple cider vinegar to cut through the thirst, and sweet honey to energize, Ginger Switchel is more than just a drink; it is a boost of love and care in liquid form. As you enjoy this humble yet invigorating drink, remember Mother Teresa and her selfless love. Just like this beverage's blend of flavors, her life was a mix of courage, dedication, and empathy. We can also quench the thirst—physical and spiritual—of those around us with love, care, and determination to keep going.

Saint Teresa of Calcutta, pray for us!

Ginger Switchel

Ingredients

(SERVES 8 TO 10)

4 tablespoons unfiltered apple cider vinegar

6 tablespoons raw honey or blackstrap molasses

1 (4-inch) piece of fresh ginger root, peeled and finely minced

8 cups water

Juice and zest of 1 fresh lime

Tools Checklist

Measuring cups
Measuring spoons
Vegetable peeler
Knife
Zester or small grater
Large jar with lid
Strainer

Instructions

1. Mix all ingredients in a large jar, cover, and shake well.
2. Put the covered jar in the refrigerator (see note).
3. To serve, strain out the ginger and pour the switchel into a glass filled with ice. Drink it straight (for a bolder, spicier flavor) or top it with still or sparkling water to dilute and soften the flavor. Stir before drinking.
4. Keep covered in the refrigerator for up to 7 days.

Note: You can drink the switchel once it is cold, or you can let the ginger infuse for up to 4 days before serving. The longer the ginger infuses, the stronger the flavor will become.

Saint Maximilian Kolbe

Mary's Knight

1894–1941 * Feast day: August 14

Patron of those addicted to drugs, those with eating disorders, families, journalists, amateur radio operators, prisoners, and the pro-life movement

Raymond Kolbe was only twelve years old when he had a vision of the Virgin Mary. She offered him a white crown, representing purity, and a red crown, representing martyrdom. He chose both, which was a foreshadowing of his life to come. From that moment, he knew his life would be dedicated to something greater—a life full of bravery, love, and faith.

One year after his vision, Kolbe and his older brother joined the Conventual Franciscans, where he took the name Maximilian. He dedicated his life to spreading the love of God through writing, publishing, and missionary work. He founded a movement called the Militia of the Immaculata, aimed at bringing people closer to Jesus through the intercession of Mary. His zeal for his mission led him to establish a large monastery in his home country of Poland and, later, another in Japan, where he used modern means like radio and printing to share the gospel.

But the most incredible part of Father Kolbe's story happened during World War II, when he was arrested by the Nazis for helping Jewish refugees. Sent to the terrible Auschwitz concentration camp, Father Kolbe continued to care for others, even though he was suffering too. One day, when a prisoner escaped, the Nazis decided to starve ten men as punishment. Hearing the cries of one of the chosen men, who feared for his family, Father Kolbe volunteered to take his place. The Nazis accepted his offer, and Father Kolbe spent his final days in the starvation bunker, leading prayers and comforting the others until he died on August 14, 1941.

To remember St. Maximilian Kolbe's incredible courage and selflessness, enjoy these Cream Cheese Stuffed Bagel Bites. Bagels, originally a Jewish food from the Polish city of Krakow, remind us of shared bonds across different cultures and the importance of helping others, just like Maximilian did.

Saint Maximilian Kolbe, pray for us!

Cream Cheese Stuffed Bagel Bites

Ingredients

(MAKES 8)

1 cup all-purpose flour
2 teaspoons baking powder
½ teaspoon salt
1 cup plain Greek yogurt
4 ounces cream cheese, cut into 8 cubes
1 egg white, whisked
Everything bagel seasoning, for sprinkling (see note)

Tools Checklist

Baking sheet
Parchment paper
Measuring cups
Measuring spoons
Medium and small bowls
Mixing spoons
Whisk
Pastry brush
Oven mitts

Instructions

1. Preheat the oven to 375°F and line a baking sheet with parchment paper.
2. Mix the flour, baking powder, and salt together in a bowl. Add the Greek yogurt and stir with a large spoon until a sticky dough forms. You'll know it's ready when the dough pulls away from the sides of the bowl.
3. Divide the dough into eight balls of equal size. Sprinkle some flour over your work area and lightly flour your hands. Place the dough balls on your work area and flatten each one evenly. Place a cube of cream cheese in the center of each flattened dough ball, then fold up the sides of the dough to seal the cream cheese in. Make sure the dough is sealed all the way around so the cream cheese does not burst out during baking.
4. Place the dough balls on the lined baking sheet and brush each with the whisked egg white. Sprinkle seasoning on top of each dough ball and bake until golden brown, around 25 minutes.
5. Let the bagel bites cool slightly before serving.

Note: To make these bagel bites a sweet snack, sprinkle the tops with cinnamon and sugar instead of everything bagel seasoning.

Saint Pier Giorgio Frassati

A Man of the Beatitudes

1901–1925 * Feast day: July 4

Patron of students, young adults, and World Youth Day

Saint Pier Giorgio Frassati lived the beatitudes with every breath. Born in Turin, Italy, in 1901, he had a joyful spirit and a deep love for others. Though he came from a wealthy family, his true riches were his faith and his love for the poor. Pier Giorgio gave freely, whether it was his bus fare, his shoes, or his time to help those in need. He considered it a privilege to serve others.

His charity wasn't just about giving material things; it was about sharing his whole heart and soul. His deep compassion was nourished by daily Communion with Christ and frequent nocturnal adoration, which was the foundation of everything he did.

In addition to his devotion, Pier Giorgio was full of life and laughter. He was known for his practical jokes and natural leadership. He guided his friends back on track when they lost their way and often gave them rosaries as gifts, leading them to Mass and prayer during outings.

Mountain climbing was one of Pier Giorgio's favorite activities, serving as both a physical challenge and a spiritual journey. He saw each climb as a chance to get closer to God, and he invited his friends to join him. His famous phrase, "to the heights," wasn't just about climbing mountains; it was about aiming high in faith and giving our hearts fully to God.

To honor Saint Pier Giorgio Frassati's love for both physical and spiritual heights, enjoy these "To the Heights" Granola Bars. Just as Pier Giorgio always aimed to climb higher—both in his faith and on the mountains—these granola bars remind us to fuel our own journeys with the same perseverance and devotion.

Saint Pier Giorgio Frassati, pray for us!

"To the Heights" Granola Bars

Ingredients

(MAKES 12)

4 tablespoons coconut oil
1/4 cup brown sugar, packed
1/3 cup honey
1/2 teaspoon vanilla extract
2 cups old-fashioned oats
2 cups crispy rice cereal
1/2 teaspoon salt
1/4 cup mini chocolate chips

Tools Checklist

8 x 8-inch baking dish
Parchment paper
Measuring cups
Measuring spoons
Small saucepan
Mixing spoons
Large bowl

Instructions

1. Line an 8 x 8-inch baking dish with parchment paper (see note).
2. In a small saucepan over medium heat, melt the coconut oil, brown sugar, and honey together. Stir until the sugar is dissolved.
3. Bring the mixture to a gentle simmer and let it bubble for 1 to 2 minutes, then add the vanilla extract. Remove from the heat to cool slightly.
4. In a large bowl, combine the oats with the rice cereal and salt. Pour the slightly cooled honey mixture over the oat mixture and stir to coat.
5. When the granola mixture is no longer hot to the touch, stir in the chocolate chips. Spoon the granola mixture into the baking dish, then use another piece of parchment paper to press it down firmly (so it won't stick to your hands).
6. Chill for an hour before cutting the mixture into 12 bars. Store at room temperature.

Note: Lining the baking dish with parchment paper makes it easy to remove the uncut granola bars from the pan when it's time to cut them.

Saint Elizabeth Ann Seton

A Champion of Education

1774–1821 * Feast day: January 4

Patron of Catholic schools, educators, those who have lost parents, widows, orphans, and those rejected or persecuted for their faith

Elizabeth Ann Seton was a remarkable woman who became the first American-born saint. Born in New York City in 1774, Elizabeth grew up in a well-off family and grew up with everything she needed. But her life took a dramatic turn when her husband, William Seton, fell ill, and the family's finances crumbled.

When her husband passed away in 1803 while they were in Italy, Elizabeth found herself a young widow with five children to care for. However, she had discovered the Catholic Church during their time in Italy, and she never lost her trust in God. When she returned to New York, Elizabeth converted to Catholicism. This decision caused many in her social circle to stop associating with her, but she remained steadfast in her new faith.

Driven by her deep love for God and a desire to help others, Elizabeth moved to Maryland, where she founded the first free Catholic school for girls in the United States. She believed in the power of education and worked tirelessly to provide a good education for children, regardless of their background. Her work didn't stop there; she also founded the Sisters of Charity, the first American religious community for women. This group dedicated themselves to teaching and caring for the poor, continuing Elizabeth's mission of service.

Saint Elizabeth Ann Seton's life teaches us about resilience, faith, and the importance of helping others. This Buttermilk Ranch Dressing and Dip is perfect to turn ordinary veggies or a salad into a flavorful afterschool snack. Let it remind you of St. Elizabeth's example of turning life's challenges into opportunities to serve others with love.

Saint Elizabeth Ann Seton, pray for us!

Buttermilk Ranch Dressing and Dip

Ingredients

(MAKES ABOUT 1½ CUPS)

½ cup sour cream
½ cup buttermilk
¼ cup mayonnaise
1 or 2 garlic cloves, minced
½ teaspoon salt
¼ teaspoon pepper
1½ teaspoons dried dill
¼ cup finely chopped fresh chives
2 teaspoons fresh lemon juice

Tools Checklist

Knives
Measuring cups
Measuring spoons
Medium bowl
Whisk

Instructions

1. Combine all of the ingredients in a medium bowl and whisk well. Taste and adjust seasoning if necessary.
2. Chill until ready to serve. Store in a covered jar or container in the refrigerator for up to 4 days.

Saint Thomas

From Doubt to Courage

First century * Feast day: July 3
Patron of judges and architects

Saint Thomas, one of Jesus' Twelve Apostles, is best known for his journey from doubt to deep faith. Often called "Doubting Thomas," he struggled to believe that Jesus had risen from the dead. But when Jesus appeared to Thomas and told Thomas to touch his wounds, Thomas' doubt transformed into a mighty declaration of faith: "My Lord and my God!" This moment teaches us that questioning can lead to stronger belief if we remain open to finding the truth.

After the resurrection of Jesus, Thomas became a brave missionary, traveling far from his homeland to spread the gospel. He traveled all the way to India, where he tirelessly preached about Jesus, built churches, and converted many people to Christianity. Thomas never gave up on his mission to share the Good News, even when it put his life in danger.

Saint Thomas' story is a reminder that faith can grow from the smallest seed of doubt. His courage and dedication led to the spread of Christianity in distant lands, leaving a lasting legacy. Remember how Thomas traveled far and wide to share his faith as you enjoy this Golden Milk Latte—a warm, comforting drink inspired by the spices of India. As you sip it, think about St. Thomas' journey from doubt to belief, and let it inspire you to seek the truth in your own life.

Saint Thomas, pray for us!

Saint Thomas

Golden Milk Latte

Ingredients

(SERVES 12)

2 cups milk

1 to 3 teaspoons sweetener, such as maple syrup or honey (optional)

1 teaspoon vanilla extract

1½ teaspoons ground turmeric

½ teaspoon ground cinnamon

½ teaspoon ground ginger

Pinch black pepper

Pinch fine sea salt

Tools Checklist

Measuring cups

Measuring spoons

Small saucepan

Whisk

Mixing spoons

Heatproof mugs

Instructions

1. Heat the milk in a saucepan over medium heat until nearly simmering, then whisk it briefly until frothy.
2. Add the sweetener (if using), vanilla extract, turmeric, cinnamon, ginger, black pepper, and salt to a heatproof mug. Pour the steamed milk, minus the foam, into the mug and stir until all ingredients are combined.
3. Add the foam on top and give the drink a brief stir.
4. Taste the latte and adjust the sweetness or seasoning if needed.
5. Serve warm.

See the recipe for Large-Batch Dry Golden Milk Mix on page 182.

Large-Batch Dry Golden Milk Mix

Saint Thomas' story is a reminder that faith can grow from the smallest seed of doubt.

Ingredients

1/3 cup ground turmeric
2 tablespoons ground cinnamon
2 tablespoons ground ginger
¾ teaspoon black pepper
¾ teaspoon fine sea salt

Tools Checklist

Measuring cups
Measuring spoons
Bowl or container with sealable lid
Mixing spoons

Instructions

1. Place all ingredients into a sealable bowl or container. Stir the ingredients together or cover the container and shake it until the ingredients are combined.
2. Store in a sealed container for up to 1 year.

Note: To make 1 serving, heat 8 ounces of your favorite milk in a small saucepan or in the microwave until it is warm but not boiling. Stir in 2 teaspoons of the mix until fully dissolved. Serve warm. Optional: Sweeten to taste with honey, maple syrup, or your preferred sweetener.

Saint María Antonia de Paz y Figueroa

The Road Less Traveled

1730–1799 * Feast day: March 7
Patron of missions in Argentina

María Antonia de Paz y Figueroa, lovingly known as Mama Antula, was a woman of incredible faith and determination. Born in 1730 in what is now Argentina, she lived during a time when religious life was a challenge in her region. When the Jesuits, who had been leading spiritual retreats, were expelled from South America, Mama Antula felt a deep calling to continue their work. Without hesitation, she took on the mission of spreading the Spiritual Exercises of St. Ignatius across her homeland.

Mama Antula wasn't afraid to walk the roads less traveled—literally! She journeyed on foot across the rugged and often dangerous countryside, wearing nothing but a simple black dress and sandals. Her journeys were long and difficult, but she was fueled by her unwavering faith in God. She would visit towns and villages, inviting people to participate in spiritual retreats that she organized. She built retreat houses where people could come to find peace and deepen their relationship with God. Despite the obstacles she faced, Mama Antula flourished in her work. Her deep love for God and her devotion to helping others grow in their faith inspired thousands to follow her. Her efforts helped revive the spiritual life in Argentina, and her legacy continues to inspire many today.

To honor St. María Antonia de Paz y Figueroa, enjoy this Off-the-Beaten-Path Trail Mix. Just as Mama Antula took the road less traveled to bring God's love to others, this trail mix is perfect for your own adventures, reminding you to stay strong and determined on your journey of faith.

Saint María Antonia de Paz y Figueroa, pray for us!

Off-the-Beaten-Path Trail Mix

Ingredients

(SERVES 8+)

3 cups unsweetened coconut flakes
2 cups sunflower seeds
2 cups pumpkin seeds
2 cups chopped dried pineapple
1 cup raisins
2 cups dark chocolate chips

Tools Checklist

Measuring cups
Large baking sheet
Knife
Mixing spoons
Oven mitts

Instructions

1. Preheat the oven to 350°F.
2. Place the coconut flakes, sunflower seeds, and pumpkin seeds on a large baking sheet and bake for 5 minutes or until barely toasted. Remove from the oven and let them cool completely.
3. Add the pineapple, raisins, and chocolate chips to the baking sheet and mix all the ingredients together.
4. Store in an airtight container at room temperature for up to 2 weeks.

Saint Juan Diego

The Miracle of Our Lady of Guadalupe

1474–1548 * Feast day: December 9

Patron of Indigenous people

Saint Juan Diego's story is one of simple faith and extraordinary miracles. Born in 1474 in what is now Mexico, Juan Diego was a humble man who lived a quiet life as a farmer. Although he wasn't wealthy or powerful, Juan Diego was rich in his love for God and his devotion to the Virgin Mary.

One cold December morning in 1531, while walking to Mass, Juan Diego heard beautiful music and saw a radiant figure on Tepeyac Hill. It was the Virgin Mary, who appeared to him surrounded by light and dressed in clothes as bright as the sun. She spoke to Juan Diego in his native language and asked him to tell the bishop to build a church on that very hill. Juan Diego, though humble, faithfully carried her message.

When the bishop asked for a sign to prove the apparition was real, Juan Diego returned to the hill. The Virgin Mary appeared again and instructed him to gather roses growing miraculously in the cold winter soil. Juan Diego carefully collected the flowers in his tilma, a simple cloak made of agave fiber. When he presented the roses to the bishop, they fell away to reveal the image of the Virgin Mary imprinted on the fabric of his cloak. This miraculous image, known as Our Lady of Guadalupe, became a powerful symbol of faith and unity in Mexico and is still venerated today.

To celebrate St. Juan Diego and his encounter with the Virgin Mary, enjoy a warm cup of Mexican Hot Chocolate. Just as Juan Diego's tilma carried the miraculous image of Our Lady, this rich and comforting drink, with its blend of chocolate and spices, reminds us of the warmth and sweetness of our Mother Mary.

Saint Juan Diego, pray for us!

Saint Juan Diego

Mexican Hot Chocolate

Ingredients

(SERVES 3 TO 4)

3 cups whole milk

3 tablespoons cocoa powder, plus more for serving

3 tablespoons sugar

1 teaspoon ground cinnamon

1 teaspoon vanilla extract

Pinch cayenne pepper

4 ounces bittersweet chocolate, chopped

Sweetened whipped cream or marshmallows, for serving

Tools Checklist

Measuring cups

Measuring spoons

Medium saucepan

Whisk

Mixing spoons

Heatproof mugs

Instructions

1. In a medium saucepan, whisk together the milk, cocoa powder, sugar, cinnamon, vanilla, and cayenne. Place over medium heat, occasionally stirring until steaming, about 5 minutes. Do not let the mixture boil.
2. Add the chocolate and stir until melted and smooth.
3. Pour the hot chocolate into heatproof mugs.
4. Top with whipped cream or marshmallows, sprinkle with a dusting of cocoa powder, and serve immediately.

Chef Notes

Calendar of Feast Days of Saints in this Book

January

January 4: Saint Elizabeth Ann Seton

January 6: Saint André Bessette

January 20: Blessed Cyprian Michael Tansi

January 20: Saint Sebastian

January 24: Saint Francis de Sales

February

February 1: Saint Brigid of Ireland

February 6: Saint Dorothy

February 6: Saint Paul Miki and companions

February 8: Saint Josephine Bakhita

February 10: Saint José Luis Sánchez del Río

March

March 3: Saint Katharine Drexel

March 7: Saints Felicity and Perpetua

March 7: Saint María Antonia de Paz y Figueroa

March 17: Saint Patrick

March 21: Saint Nicholas of Flüe

April

April 16: Saint Bernadette

May

May 3: Saints Timothy and Maura

May 4: Saint Florian

May 11: Saint Anthony of Saint Ann Galvão

May 15: Saint Isidore the Farmer

May 16: Saint Brendan the Navigator

May 26: Saint Philip Neri

May 30: Saint Joan of Arc

June

June 3: Saint Charles Lwanga and companions

June 22: Saint Thomas More

June 24: Saint John the Baptist

July

July 1: Saint Junipero Serra

July 3: Saint Thomas

July 4: Saint Pier Giorgio Frassati

July 7: Blessed Peter To Rot

July 11: Saint Benedict

July 12: Saints Louis and Zélie Martin

July 13: Saint Teresa of the Andes

July 14: Saint Kateri Tekakwitha

July 22: Saint Anna Wang

July 29: Saint Martha

August

August 1: Saint Alphonsus Liguori

August 10: Saint Lawrence

August 14: Saint Maximilian Kolbe

August 18: Saint Helena

August 23: Saint Bartholomew

August 23: Saint Rose of Lima

August 28: Saint Augustine

September

September 5: Saint Teresa of Calcutta

September 17: Saint Hildegard of Bingen

September18: Saint Joseph of Cupertino

September 20: Saint Andrew Kim Taegon

September 21: Saint Matthew

September 23: Saint Padre Pio

September 29: Saint Michael the Archangel

October

October 1: Saint Thérèse of Lisieux

October 5: Saint Faustina Kowalska

October 12: Saint Carlo Acutis

October 15: Saint Teresa of Ávila

October 21: Saint Laura Montoya

October 25: Saints Crispin and Crispinian

November

November 3: Saint Martin de Porres

November 16: Saint Margaret of Scotland

November 17: Saint Elizabeth of Hungary

November 22: Saint Cecilia

November 24: Saint Andrew Dũng-Lạc and companions

November 30: Saint Andrew

December

December 9: Venerable Fulton Sheen

December 9: Saint Juan Diego

December 13: Saint Lucy

December 23: Saint Thorlak of Iceland

No Feast Day

Venerable Emil Kapaun (died on May 23)

Chef Notes

About the Author

Shelby Siegfried is a Catholic writer living on the Nebraska prairie with her husband, Cody, and their five kids. She holds a degree in agricultural communications and journalism from Kansas State University. She spends her time juggling writing projects, cooking from scratch, and soaking up the noise, laughter, and backyard adventures that make up the beautiful chaos of family life.

About the Illustrator

Ted Schluenderfritz has illustrated many children's books, including *The Narrow Gate* and *Rejoice and Be Glad* (written by his wife, Rachel), *Portrait of the Son* by Josephine Nobisso, the Old and New series by Maura Roan McKeegan,

The Holy Spirit and the Greatest Adventure by Gracia Jagla, and *The Attic Saint* by Tim Drake. You can view his work at 5sparrows.com and @schluenderfritz on Instagram.